THE COMPLETE GUIDE TO SMOKING MEAT

The Complete Guide to Smoking Meat

100 Smokin' Good Recipes for BBQ and More

DERRICK RICHES *and* SABRINA BAKSH

PHOTOGRAPHY BY IAIN BAGWELL

ROCKRIDGE PRESS

For general information on our other products and services or to obtain technical support, please contact our Customer Care Department within the United States at (866) 744-2665, or outside the United States at (510) 253-0500.

Rockridge Press publishes its books in a variety of electronic and print formats. Some content that appears in print may not be available in electronic books, and vice versa.

Interior and Cover Designer: Sean Doyle
Art Producer: Sara Feinstein
Editor: Anna Pulley
Production Editor: Holland Baker
Production Managers: Michael Kay, Sandy Noman

Paperback ISBN: 978-1-63807-107-5
eBook ISBN: 978-1-63807-969-9
R0

For Zoë

CONTENTS

INTRODUCTION

The discovery of fire led to the invention of cooking. That first meal was likely flavored with smoke. Since then, humans have had an affinity for the taste of wood-fired foods. Today we have a variety of grills, smokers, and other cooking equipment that can add smoke flavor to any food item we wish. This book teaches you how to do just that—infuse that delicious, smoky flavor into every meal.

Derrick Riches has written about outdoor cooking since 1997, and he has cooked on every conceivable type of equipment, from the most expensive grills and smokers to a pile of coals in the ground. Sabrina Baksh has explored the world of live-fire cooking using a global culinary perspective. Together, we bring our experience and know-how to help you add a little (or a lot of) smoke to any foods you cook.

While this book primarily focuses on animal proteins, we have also added a wide array of fruit- and vegetable-based dishes to the mix. Many people think of meat when firing up the grill or the smoker, but as you'll see in this book, you can prepare entire meals—veggies and side dishes as well—with a delicious, smoky flavor. We will cover everything from traditional low and slow barbecue to hot and fast dishes. After all, the temperature setting does not limit the amount of smoke that can be added to the food.

To keep things simple, every recipe in this book can be made using either a grill or a smoker. One item to mention: This book does not include any cold-smoking methods or recipes. Cold smoking is entirely different from hot smoking and requires special equipment and advanced skills to do it safely.

Our goal is to help you learn the basics of smoking. Once you have mastered the basic skills, you can take them further and pursue more complicated techniques and recipes. We have included information on how to ramp up your smoking game, whether you're cooking your first brisket, learning how to use an injection marinade, or making the perfect candied salmon or smoked game bird. Whether you are new to outdoor cooking or are an experienced backyard cook, there is a method, trick, or recipe in this book for everyone. So, fire up your grill, grab some smoking wood, and let's get cooking!

CHAPTER 1

SMOKING FUNDAMENTALS

SMOKING as we know it today evolved from ancient traditions, beginning as a process for preserving meats and fish for the long winters and becoming a popular outdoor activity and a mainstay of our modern-day patio culture. Recently, cooking with smoke has become something of a phenomenon. Smokers and grills are more accessible today than ever before, and many supermarkets carry wood pellets, chunks, planks, and almost anything else you need to add smoke to everything you cook.

The basic process for smoking is similar in many ways to roasting or baking. You use an enclosed, heated chamber for cooking, either at a high temperature quickly or at a low temperature slowly. If you imagine this process is just like cooking in your oven, all you need to learn is how to add smoke. That's what this book is all about.

To add smoke correctly, you need the right kind of wood to generate it. There is a wide range of wood "flavors" to choose from, including heavy and robust to light and sweet, and everything in between. Next, consider the cooking equipment. Whether you own a big smoking rig or a small gas grill, there are strategies you can use to produce a good dose of smoke. Once you master a few basics, which we'll cover in this chapter, you will be able to smoke the perfect barbecue brisket, holiday turkey, or weeknight salmon fillet, plus delicious appetizers and side dishes to make the meal.

WHY WE LOVE THE TASTE OF SMOKE

There is just something about the flavor of smoke. Whether you grew up with traditional barbecue, spend your summers cooking by a campfire, or enjoy smoked fish or meats as snacks on road trips, most of us have an affinity for food cooked over wood.

A lot of people think of barbecue when they think of smoked foods. And while you'll find plenty of recipes for brisket, ribs, and pork in the chapters that follow, there's so much more to smoking. Many foods benefit from a simple kiss (or a heavy dose) of smoke. From quickly smoked fish fillets to a low and slow turkey, cooking with smoke makes everything taste better.

Think of jerky, smoked salmon, or a smoky potato casserole. Now think about the s'mores you've made over a campfire. We have you covered for all these and more. So many classic foods enjoyed for generations have had that touch of smoke, and today we have the equipment, the wood, and the know-how to do it right.

Not All Smoke Is Created Equal

The smoke needed to cook food is very specific. Fortunately, it isn't difficult to achieve, but you need to know what to expect. Smoke can be powerful, so it needs to flow properly around the food. It should be generated by hot, fast combustion even if you're cooking low and slow. This is what provides the much-sought-after thin blue smoke.

Smoke that is dark gray or black will give your food a bitter, tongue-numbing flavor. Slowly billowing white smoke can make for a stale aroma coming out of your cooker. Worst of all, both of these can indicate a buildup of creosote. This thick, tar-like substance is produced by smoke that lingers too long and comes from a source that may be tainted with resins, lighter fluid, or charcoal additives.

The thin blue smoke is a pitmaster's dream. It indicates the fuel is burning efficiently and cleanly. You can achieve this with the right fire, the right fuel, and the right airflow. We will address the specifics of this in the sections to come.

Smoking at Any Temperature

You've probably heard about the barbecue joint that smokes its brisket for more than 20 hours. For traditional barbecue, the secret has always been low and slow. It involves the precision of fire control and a lot of patience. Of course, many pieces of cooking equipment can take the guesswork out of the process, but knowing the fundamentals will help you be a better cook.

At the other end of the spectrum from low and slow is hot and fast cooking. For a perfectly seared steak, you may want to go as hot as possible to achieve the right texture and doneness. Likewise, a dose of smoke can add flavor without overpowering the meat. When it comes to finding the right temperature, you need to understand the food you're working with and what you'd like the results to be.

Low and slow cooking encourages the breakdown of collagen, which transforms tough cuts of meat into fork-tender morsels. This is not ideal, however, for a fillet of fish or a high-quality steak. You might want these items smoky, but too much cooking time can yield a dry, inedible piece of meat. Smaller, more delicate foods should start with a burst of smoke, just like adding a dash of seasoning.

A QUICK GUIDE TO SMOKERS

Most outdoor cooking equipment can produce a smoky flavor; some just do it better than others. The recipes in this book work with most types of cookers. If you are serious about your smoking journey, though, we recommend purchasing a smoker. Following is a breakdown of the types of smokers currently available on the market.

Bullet/Water Smoker

These charcoal-fired cookers are simple and inexpensive. They might take a few attempts to master, but they produce incredible smoked foods. The units have the advantage of being smaller, and the interior water pan adds moisture and balances heat. This feature provides a consistent temperature without having to fiddle with vents or controls. Once mastered, a good vertical water smoker can run for 20 hours without any attention.

Offset Smoker

A classic barbecue staple, the offset smoker has a large cooking chamber and a connected fire chamber. It keeps the fire away from the food so it can maintain low and slow temperatures. These units are typically made from heavy-gauge steel and can require some practice to master, but the results are worth the time spent. This style of smoker is used in barbecue competitions and in some of the best barbecue joints in the world. We don't recommend the budget versions of these smokers since their temperatures can be uneven.

Kamado Grill

A kamado grill is an excellent smoker as well as a fantastic grill. These units can easily hold temperatures of 200°F to 700°F with only minor adjustments to the vents. Normally the grills are made of a ceramic material, causing them to be very energy efficient. To properly smoke on a kamado unit, you will need a diffuser plate (sometimes called a plate setter) to act as a divider between the fire and the food. These grills carry a higher price tag, but they may be worth it for their fuel efficiency.

Wood Pellet Grill

Pellet grills have exploded on the market, becoming the must-have backyard cooker. And for good reason: They are incredibly easy smokers to operate. Pellet grills sometimes struggle to reach temperatures above 500°F, but for smoking, they are hard to beat. Many of these grills have Wi-Fi–enabled controls that allow you to monitor and control the grill from your smartphone or other device. Pellet cookers are available in both a standard horizontal grill configuration and a vertical smoker design.

Electric Smoker

Electric smokers are some of the most affordable cookers on the market. They use an electric heating element placed under a pan of wood chips to produce smoke. The thermostat controls the temperature, so you really can set it and forget it. The biggest drawback with electric smokers is their low smoke production when set to low cooking temperatures. Even at higher temperatures, you may have to add more wood chips every few hours to achieve the flavor you're looking for.

Gas Smoker

Like electric smokers, these units generally have a dial to adjust the temperature, but instead of a heating element, these smokers use a gas burner. This burner heats a pan filled with wood chips to produce smoke. The advantage they have over their electric cousins is that they can deliver more heat. You will need a propane tank to connect to the unit, since very few gas smokers are available for use with natural gas hookups.

THE TWO-ZONE FIRE

Grilling is hot and fast and happens close to the flame. It is the perfect cooking method for a steak or any other item that cooks quickly. But most other foods need to be cooked indirectly. We call this indirect method the "two-zone fire." What this means is that the fire is on one side of the grill and the food is on the other side. You should be able to look straight down onto the cooking grates and see all the fire, all the food, and a small space between them.

Two-Zone Setup for a Charcoal Grill

Building a two-zone fire in a charcoal grill is easy. Light your charcoal and get it burning to the point where it has a fine white surface layer. Now bank all the coals to one side of the grill. Position the cooking grate, then place the food on the side opposite the direct flame. Once the lid is in place, the heat will fill the chamber, cooking the food without the direct heat drying it out.

A charcoal chimney is indispensable in charcoal cooking. This lighting device allows you to start heating the charcoal separately, outside the grill, and then pour the coals exactly where you need them. Chimneys are particularly useful if you need to light additional charcoal to add later on when using a long cook time.

LUMP CHARCOAL VS. BRIQUETTES

Charcoal briquettes are made from sawdust and a binding agent. They are pressed into a pillow shape and fired to make charcoal. Lump charcoal is made from wood scraps (either from lumber mills or tree branch pieces) fired in a kiln that reduces it to charcoal.

So which kind of charcoal is best? The truth is, it can depend on the brand. Briquettes are very uniform and will give you consistency. Lump charcoal tends to burn hotter but can be a bit hit-or-miss. Many hardcore barbecue cooks prefer lump because it offers a cleaner burn with less ash production. Also, briquettes have additives (usually sucrose) to bind them. We leave the choice to you, since the differences are not overwhelming. We do recommend avoiding self-lighting charcoal, which produces an undesirable flavor, especially during long cooking times.

Two-Zone Setup for a Gas Grill

Configuring your gas grill for a two-zone fire is simple. Depending on how many burners your grill has, simply turn on the burners that are opposite the food you will be cooking. If your grill has only two burners, or isn't large enough to set aside room for the food, you will need to rotate the food every hour to maintain even cooking.

MASTERING THE FIRE

Getting your grill to its highest temperature setting is simple. With gas, you simply turn it to high. With charcoal, you build a big fire and let it go. Maintaining a lower temperature for smoking, however, may not be as intuitive. Gas grills have knobs labeled with helpful high, medium, and low indications, letting you experiment with finding a steady 250°F. Once you know the settings, you are ready to cook.

Charcoal requires a different approach, though. With charcoal, we need to control the fire. This means putting on the lid and adjusting the vents so that the grill will hold the target temperature. Every time you lift the lid, you let out heat and let in oxygen. This causes the temperature to drop, jump, and then stabilize. Don't panic. This is normal; it is how low and slow cooking has been done for decades.

That said, there's room for variability. When a recipe says to smoke at 225°F, that's meant to be an average temperature. Of course, if your fire jumps over 300°F for more than 20 or 30 minutes, you might have a problem. However, a properly set charcoal grill should hold a stable temperature for several hours.

When cooking with charcoal, start with a big fire. You want a lot of charcoal burning, and when the coals are burning cleanly, put the grill lid on and close the vents to achieve your target temperature. If you are cooking for more than 6 to 8 hours, you might need to add additional fuel. In this case, use a charcoal chimney to light more charcoal and add it to the grill when the initial charcoal has burned down to one-third its original size. It is always better to add additional fuel early rather than later in the cooking process.

KEEP IT DRY

When burning wood for smoke, you want the combustion to be clean and steady. What you don't want is a steamy, smoldering smoke that provides little aroma. For that reason, don't soak your wood chips and chunks. Yes, that has been the advice for a generation, but it does nothing but lead to poor smoke production.

Whatever form of wood you use, it should be dry. In fact, it should be stored carefully to ensure it stays dry. In even moderately humid environments, dry wood will absorb moisture from the air, which can cause mold to grow on the wood and lead to bad smoke. So keep your smoking wood in an airtight container until you are ready to use it.

The Fuel

The best way to achieve good smoke is with the right kind of wood. For smoking, you want to use clean and dry hardwood. You can find a variety of smoking chips, chunks, and pellets in many grocery stores or home improvement stores.

Chips vs. chunks: Wood chips are small pieces of hardwood. They look very much like wood shavings. They burn fast and are good for quick, short bursts of smoke. In general, when smoking for periods longer than 1 hour, we recommend chunks (large chunks, if you can find them). These will burn slowly, producing consistent smoke for longer periods. You might want to add additional wood chunks every hour or two depending on how fast you burn through them.

Food-grade wood pellets: Wood pellets are compressed sawdust. They burn quickly, producing a lot of smoke in a short period of time.

Alternative smoke sources: There are several other fuels you can use to produce smoke. Dried corn cobs are a favorite in the Midwest for smoking pork. In the South, you will find many people using pecan shells; they produce mild smoke and are excellent for quick cook times. Dried grapevines can also be used.

WOOD PELLETS

With the explosion in the popularity of pellet grills, food-grade wood pellets are widely available. Even if you don't have a pellet grill, you can use wood pellets for producing smoke in any grill or smoker. The pellets burn easily, create plenty of smoke, and come in a variety of flavors. Wood pellets can be more budget-friendly than wood chips or chunks, owing to their high production volume.

Be selective, however, when buying wood pellets. Many brands of wood pellets are not exactly what they say they are. Wood pellets contain sawdust, and the facilities that make them are usually located near major logging companies. Depending on the forest they are near, these pellets can contain random types of wood, which is then flavored and colored.

If you are interested in a specific flavor profile for your smoke, we recommend seeking out a reputable brand of wood pellets that don't have added flavor and are actually made from the wood listed on the bag.

Smoke Flavors

There is a lot of attention paid to the flavors that different woods can produce in your food, but a lot of this is more about marketing than actual taste. This is not to say that certain woods don't have distinct flavors. Still, most people will probably not distinguish between cherry, apple, or maple woods—the flavor differences are far too subtle. While we like to make recommendations based on years of experience, your personal preference should always come first in any recipe's suggested wood type. In the chart that follows, we offer a simplified breakdown of the flavors of smoke.

TYPES OF WOOD

WOOD	INTENSITY	DESCRIPTION
ALDER	Moderate	This is not actually hardwood, but it is the traditional wood of the Pacific Northwest's hot smoked salmon.
APPLE, CHERRY, MAPLE, PECAN, PEACH	Mild	The go-to general-purpose wood for mild smoke flavor.
OAK	Moderate/Strong	This is the classic wood for barbecue. Use this wood with beef, lamb, or pork.
HICKORY	Strong	Another classic for barbecue cooking, particularly pork. This wood provides a robust smoke flavor.
MESQUITE	Very Strong	Mesquite is also not a hardwood. Good for fish and other short cook times, this wood is high in resins and used for short bursts of smoke.

Smoking on a Charcoal Grill

Most charcoal grills can be set up as a functional smoker. The grill must be large enough that the item you intend to smoke takes up less than half the cooking area. Build your charcoal fire under one side of the cooking grate and place the food over the unheated section. To make it even more efficient, place an aluminum pan under the food to collect drippings and a second pan filled with water over the fire. You have now built a small water smoker. Wood chunks are added directly to the burning charcoal.

You might need to add additional fuel to the fire for long cooking times. It's best not to add charcoal straight from the bag to a fire. Even the best-quality lump charcoal should be burning before it is used for smoking. This eliminates any foul flavors that might linger in the raw charcoal. We recommend using a charcoal chimney to light the additional charcoal. Once the charcoal is burning hot, add it to the fire.

Smoking on a Gas Grill

Before you get underway, always make sure you have sufficient fuel for your gas grill. We recommend keeping a full spare fuel tank on hand if you're using a propane grill.

Using a gas grill as a smoker is a challenge. While some models have built-in smoker boxes and even dedicated smoker burners, gas grills can't hold smoke inside very well: The smoke produced in the grill flows out through the vents. You can, however, create smoke on a gas grill and cook at low and slow temperatures.

When cooking at low temperatures on a gas grill, there isn't enough heat to keep wood chips burning. Therefore, we recommend placing a smoker box (see following) directly over the burner that you will be using. Doing this helps keep the chips burning. If you can remove one of the cooking grates, you will have better access to your smoke-making equipment while cooking.

Most important, when smoking on a gas grill, cook indirectly. This means that the food is cooked away from the burners that are in use.

Other helpful tools for cooking on a gas grill include:

Smoker box: This is a small metal box with a vented lid that can be used to burn wood chips in a gas grill. If you are looking to add a smoker box to your gas grill, we recommend a cast-iron version. They hold heat better and produce better smoke, and they work best with small wood chips.

Smoke packet: A smoke packet is made by placing wood chips or pellets in a square of aluminum foil and folding up the sides to shape it into a square package. Use a knife to puncture several holes in the sides to allow air to flow in and smoke to escape.

Smoke tube: A smoke tube is a metal mesh cylinder that burns food-grade wood pellets that are ignited with a long match or lighter. The pellets burn independently, so they don't need the grill's burners to continue producing smoke. These tubes are growing in popularity, and they are not only for making smoke on a gas grill but also for any other application where you need to produce smoke without providing heat.

GETTING GREAT SMOKE FLAVOR

More isn't always better. Many people approach smoke cooking with the idea that it is entirely about the smoke. It isn't—it's about the food. Brisket should taste like beef. Spareribs should taste like pork. The smoke is a seasoning to enhance the food, not overpower it. The careful balance of moisture, seasoning, and smoke is an art. Following are our tips to maintain that balance.

Keep It Moist

A primary by-product of all combustion is water in the form of vapor. This moisture is a vital ingredient in proper smoking. Consider smoking a brisket for 20 hours, which isn't a long stretch for brisket. How does that meat not dry out? In part, it's due to the humid environment of the cooking chamber. However, we need to supplement this environment with extra moisture.

Additionally, smoke bonds with moisture in the cooking chamber and helps deposit the smoke flavor in foods. A perfectly dry cooking environment will not produce a strong smoke flavor. For this reason, it might be necessary to add a water pan to your grill or smoker. This is particularly true of cooking equipment not specifically designed for smoking, like gas or basic charcoal grills.

Place water pans close to the heat source to optimize steam production. There are water smokers that position the pan directly over the fire. This balances the heat and provides moisture. Depending on your equipment, you may or may not want to add a water pan.

Another strategy to prevent drying is using a mop or a spritz. Mops are traditionally made with fruit juices, cider vinegar, water, oil, and seasonings and are applied with a mop-like brush (hence the name). A spritz is applied using a spray bottle and contains either fruit juice or a combination of juice and cider vinegar. Look for dry portions of meat and apply the mop or spritz to that area once the bark has set. (Bark is the dark, flavorful crust that occurs when the spice rub and the smoke combine with the meat proteins through a chemical reaction.) If the meat appears moist on the surface, adding extra moisture isn't necessary.

Getting the Smoke

During long cooks, there will be a good smoke flavor produced. The meat you put in the smoker should be cold, but it doesn't have to come straight from the refrigerator. The meat absorbs smoke better at lower temperatures. As the meat cooks, it will take on less and less smoke. This is why we can wrap large cuts of meat during the later stage of smoking. Wrapping contains the moisture without affecting the smoky flavor.

For this reason, if you are adding smoke packets or smoke tubes to your cooker, we recommend adding these items at the same time as you add the food so that smoke production coincides with the first wave of heat that hits the food. During long cooking times, there will be plenty of opportunities for the food to get smoky. If you prefer a lighter smoke flavor, don't add extra wood, or use a milder wood. And consider wrapping the meat at a later stage of the cooking process. If you do wrap, plan to unwrap for the last hour to develop a good surface bark on the meat.

Smoky Strategies for Hotter and Faster

Short smoking times, like those used for many smaller items, such as fish and vegetables, may not achieve as much smoke flavor as you're looking for. But don't assume that you need to apply thick smoke production to get the flavor you're after. Mild fish, for example, will certainly reflect that smokiness when cooked hot and fast.

One strategy for intensifying the smoke flavor is to tent the food in the cooker. Place a disposable aluminum pan over the food so that it creates a secondary smoking chamber. Doing this will capture more smoke and allow it to stay in contact with the food longer. We recommend experimenting with this because, in some instances, the smoke flavor might overpower the food.

Smoke Depth

Long smokes increase the smoke flavor, and the depth of the smoke will penetrate the food. The smoke ring, a band of reddish coloring on smoked meats, is not a factor of the amount of smoke but, rather, a reaction between nitrates in the smoke and proteins in the meat. While desirable in the barbecue community, it has little bearing on flavor.

Smoke will penetrate the surface of foods, so the more surface area, the greater the smoke flavor. To reduce the smokiness of foods, keep them whole and avoid trimming away fats from the surface. To intensify the smoke flavor, remove the surface fat.

Knowing When Enough Is Enough

The level of smoke flavor to achieve is a matter of personal preference. While we have laid out a few strategies to adjust that flavor profile, a certain amount of experimentation is required to find your preferred level. For this reason, we recommend starting small. In this book, there are a few "beginner" recipes for items like brisket and pulled pork that are faster, simpler versions of barbecue classics.

We always recommend using chicken as an introduction to smoke cooking. Chicken is very forgiving, is comparatively inexpensive, and cooks quickly and easily. You might want to try smoking a whole chicken (see BBQ Whole Chicken, page 84) as your first experiment. Make sure to pay close attention to the times, temperatures, and smoking woods so you can make whatever modifications you find necessary next time. Quick mastery of simple smoked chicken will make it easier to experiment with other foods in the future.

WHEN IS IT DONE?

Low and slow cooking with smoke plays by its own rules. A beef roast is overcooked in a high-temperature oven when it reaches an internal temperature of 150°F. On the smoker, however, it's just getting started. Always use a reliable meat thermometer to test for doneness and monitor your cooking progress. And, most important, be patient. Smoking at low temperatures can follow different rules, so plan accordingly and follow the recipe.

The Importance of a Meat Thermometer

Tootsie Tomanetz, of Snow's BBQ in Lexington, Texas, is a legend of barbecue. She has cooked traditional central Texas barbecue since the 1960s and does not own a meat thermometer. She works from experience, touch, and color. When you have this level of experience, you can put down the thermometer. Until then, always temperature-check your meat. This is more than just a food safety issue. Certain cuts, recipes, or cooking styles require a good understanding of temperatures and levels of doneness. But all meat is not created equal. You may think you know the doneness of every steak you cook, but there will always be one that just behaves differently on the grill. The only way you can know for sure is by using a reliable thermometer.

Different Kinds of Done

According to USDA guidelines, the safe internal temperature of a steak is 145°F. However, a medium-rare steak is cooked to no more than 135°F. Technically speaking, if you order a medium-rare steak, you just might be putting your life at risk. That risk is tiny, but it is still there. The truth is that food safety guidelines are not about how to cook meat but, rather, how to consume it properly.

That said, when it comes to low and slow cooking, we frequently cook to temperatures well beyond these safety guidelines. Do you want a perfectly tender brisket? Look for an internal temperature of 205°F. The same goes for most things that fall under the umbrella of barbecue cooking.

Low and slow allows us to cook to levels that would be considered overcooked in any other culinary tradition. In fact, we want to cook longer when it comes to smoking. Smoke absorption is a slow process, and it needs time to develop a rich flavor. The recipes in this book are designed to give food the time and proper temperature to achieve perfect results.

The Stall

Anyone with experience smoking large cuts of meat has witnessed something called the stall. This is a period during the cooking process when the internal temperature of the meat stops rising. Typically, this occurs somewhere between 155°F and 165°F. In this range, the temperature of smoked meats can hold steady for as long as three hours, depending on the size of the cut.

Many inexperienced barbecue cooks can find this frustrating. The primary reason for the stall has to do with nothing more than the evaporation of liquids. It's basic physics. For water to turn from a liquid to a gas requires energy in the form of heat. As water evaporates from the surface of meats in the smoker, it absorbs heat from its environment. This cools the meat while it is being cooked. The net result is that smoked foods will slow their cooking process, sometimes dramatically.

As a smoke connoisseur, you'll need to be patient with this process. It is part of low and slow cooking. Connective tissues are breaking down during the stall, creating sugars, and what was a tough cut will be turning into something tender and wonderful. Simply put, don't fight the stall—just wait it out.

RESTING AND CARRYOVER HEAT

There has been some controversy of late about resting meats after cooking. The truth is that resting is important for meats, particularly, denser red meats cooked at high temperatures. Resting allows muscle fibers time to release from the intense heat, making for a more tender cut. Resting also lets large cuts of meat, like a whole brisket, chuck roast, whole turkey, or pork butt, redistribute their heat. A well-rested roast will be more tender and flavorful.

Another issue with resting is the carryover heat. Thicker cuts cook unevenly, with the exterior reaching much higher temperatures than the center. Always test for doneness in the center or the thickest part of the meat. By resting larger pieces of meat, you let the temperature even out and allow juices to distribute from the center to the exterior. As the heat spreads, the center temperature will continue to climb. The larger the food item, the more the temperature will rise.

We've included resting times for most recipes, but as a rule of thumb, rest your steaks for 5 to 10 minutes. A large roast, like a brisket or a pork butt, should rest for at least 30 minutes. To properly rest meats, cover them with aluminum foil and then with a kitchen towel. This holds in heat and protects the meat from drying out in the open air. You can rest larger cuts on a cooking tray in your oven (turned off). This will keep in the heat and prevent air from flowing around the meat, robbing it of moisture.

THE RECIPES

The recipes in this book offer amazing meal options and will guide you through each item's smoking process, inspiring you for future cookouts. We have included a mixture of classic barbecue and smoked side dishes, featuring a wide selection of meats, fish, and poultry. Master these easy-to-follow recipes, and you'll be ready to take on more complicated ones in no time. All the recipes have been tested and reflect years of experience with live-fire cooking. We hope you enjoy every single one! To make things simpler, each recipe includes the following information:

Servings: Portion sizes can be subjective. We provide this information so you can plan accordingly.

Prep time: This refers to the time it will take you to prepare the food for cooking.

Cook time: This is the estimated time a recipe needs to cook. We cook to temperature, not time, so use this as a guide, not a rule. The recipes will also tell you the target temperature of the food you are cooking. And because some recipes require cooking by some other method in addition to the smoking, the cook time includes this time in the total. With a few rare exceptions, the cook time does not include the resting time after cooking.

Suggested wood: The wood you use to create smoke is your choice, but we include suggestions to guide you through each selection. When you are familiar with the flavor profile of each wood, you will find your favorites.

Before beginning the recipes, we suggest you review the information on grill and smoker types, as methods vary depending on equipment. Each recipe also includes a SmokeMaster Tip or a Variation suggestion. These give you little tidbits of information to ramp up your smoking skills and help you make the most of your low and slow cooking experience.

Bratwursts with Smoked Sauerkraut, 71

CHAPTER 2

BEEF, LAMB, AND VENISON

BEGINNER'S BRISKET

PREP TIME: 15 minutes / **Cook time:** 4 hours 15 minutes to 5 hours 20 minutes

A full-size brisket can take 15 to 20 hours to reach perfect tenderness. This recipe keeps it as simple as possible and is perfect for the beginner as well as those looking to prepare a smaller meal. If you have some extra time and want to make the flavor of the brisket really shine, marinate it for 12 to 24 hours in the Brisket Injection Marinade (page 169) after trimming any loose pieces from the brisket and before smoking it. After the brisket has been marinated, follow the recipe as directed beginning with step 2 (omitting the salt and pepper seasoning).

SERVES 6 TO 8

SUGGESTED WOOD: Oak, Apple, Cherry

- 1 (5- to 6-pound) brisket flat
- 2 tablespoons coarse salt
- 1 tablespoon freshly ground black pepper
- ¼ cup beef broth

SMOKEMASTER TIP: The secret to reheating smoked food is to do it low and slow, just like it was originally cooked. To reheat this small brisket flat, wrap it tightly in aluminum foil and place it in the oven at 250°F until warmed through—140°F is sufficient. Avoid overwarming since it doesn't need to be cooked twice.

1. Trim any loose pieces of meat or fat from the brisket. Season all surfaces evenly with salt and pepper.
2. Preheat the grill or smoker to 225°F. Depending on your cooker type, have ready your choice of wood chunks or smoke packets while the grill comes to temperature.
3. Place the brisket on the indirect side of the cooking grate, add wood chunks or smoke packets, and close the lid.
4. Let the brisket smoke for 3 hours, or until the internal temperature of the meat reaches 160°F.
5. Remove the brisket from the smoker and place it on a large sheet of aluminum foil. Pour the beef broth over top of the brisket and fold up the sides of the foil, sealing the brisket tightly. Return the wrapped brisket to the smoker.

6. Continue cooking for 1 to 2 hours, or until the internal temperature of the brisket reaches 190°F. Remove from the foil and return to the smoker for an additional 15 to 20 minutes, or until the internal temperature reaches 195° to 200°F.

7. Remove the brisket from the smoker, cover loosely with foil, and let the brisket rest for 15 to 20 minutes. Carve against the grain and serve.

Brisket Basics

Brisket is considered the most challenging of barbecue's traditional cuts. A full packer brisket can weigh up to 20 pounds and require 1 hour of smoking time per pound to reach perfect tenderness. The brisket is, in fact, two different muscles combined in one cut. The large, thin section–called the flat–runs the length of the cut, while the rounded section–called the point–sits on top.

To get the most out of a smoked brisket, there are a few things you need to understand. The meat is kept moist during the cooking process not by the large fat sections but by the intramuscular fat between the muscle fibers. Excess fat, including the fat cap on top of the brisket, slows the cooking process, so we recommend trimming away the bulk of the exterior fat, leaving ¼ inch on the meat.

Even with a large amount of intramuscular fat, a brisket can dry out during the long cook time. Spritzing the brisket with liquid during the second half of the cooking time will add extra moisture. Use either apple cider vinegar for a slight tartness or a mixture of equal parts apple juice and water for a sweeter flavor.

Another strategy is to wrap the brisket with butcher paper once it reaches an internal temperature of around 165°F. This method is often referred to as the Texas Crutch. Wrapping with butcher paper instead of aluminum foil allows the brisket to breathe during this phase of the cook and produces a better bark and color. After the brisket has reached an internal temperature of 200°F, remove it from the grill. Leave it wrapped to hold in the juices, and place in a warm location to rest for up to 1 hour.

To properly carve a brisket, separate the flat from the point. Carve the flat into ¼-inch-thick slices from end to end, cutting across the grain. Cube the point section into 1-inch bites.

SANTA MARIA TRI-TIP

PREP TIME: 20 minutes / **Cook time:** 2 to 2½ hours

Beef tri-tip roast is the go-to meat for Santa Maria barbecue. In this recipe, we use a more complex spice blend rather than the usual salt and pepper. The meat is slow-smoked and then pulled off the smoker as soon as it reaches the optimal internal temperature, resulting in a deeply rich, perfectly smoked tri-tip. If you can't find ancho chile powder, feel free to use regular chili powder.

SERVES 6

SUGGESTED WOOD: Oak

1 (4- to 5-pound) tri-tip roast
2 tablespoons brown sugar
1½ teaspoons smoked paprika
1½ teaspoons kosher salt
1 teaspoon onion powder
1 teaspoon ancho chile powder
½ teaspoon granulated garlic
½ teaspoon freshly ground black pepper
½ teaspoon cayenne pepper

1. Preheat the grill or smoker to 225°F. Depending on your cooker type, add your choice of wood chips or smoke packet to the fire.
2. Trim any excess fat from the roast's surface. In a small bowl, combine the brown sugar, smoked paprika, salt, onion powder, chile powder, granulated garlic, black pepper, and cayenne pepper. Apply the rub to the meat and let it stand at room temperature for 15 minutes.
3. Place the roast into the grill or smoker, close the lid, and cook for 2 to 2½ hours, or until the internal temperature at the thickest part of the meat reaches 130°F.
4. Remove the tri-tip and transfer to a cutting board, then tent with aluminum foil. Let it rest for 10 to 15 minutes before carving.

SMOKEMASTER TIP: It is important to slice a tri-tip roast correctly. There are two pointed corners. Find the crook between the two corners and separate the roast. Slice from the smallest point to the largest edge on both portions. Doing this will give you moist and tender pieces.

CENTRAL TEXAS BARBECUE BRISKET

PREP TIME: 20 minutes / **Cook time:** 14 to 16 hours

In barbecue cooking, brisket is king. While it can be challenging, it can also be the most rewarding cut of meat to smoke. This Central Texas Barbecue Brisket is slow smoked with simple seasonings to let the flavor of the beef and the smoke shine through. Patience and a steady, slow heat are the real pitmaster secrets for this brisket.

SERVES 12 TO 14

SUGGESTED WOOD:
Oak, Hickory

1 (12- to 14-pound) whole packer beef brisket
¼ cup coarse salt
¼ cup freshly ground black pepper
Butcher paper or aluminum foil

1. Pat the brisket dry with paper towels and place it on a large cutting board, flat-side down. (The point is rounded and thicker, and the flat is larger and thinner.) Using a sharp knife, score the thinnest portion of the brisket. The meat should be a minimum of 1 inch in thickness. Remove large sections of fat from the brisket, including any membrane.

2. In a small bowl, combine the salt and pepper and apply the mixture evenly over the entire surface of the brisket. Set aside, allowing the meat to absorb the salt and pepper, while you preheat the grill or smoker.

3. Preheat smoker to 225°F. Depending on your cooker type, add some of your preferred wood chunks or smoke packet to the fire. Plan for a 14-hour cook time. If you are using a grill or other cooker, make sure you cook using indirect heat.

4. Place the brisket on the smoker, close the lid, and cook until it has reached an internal temperature of around 160°F (about 8 hours), then remove the brisket and wrap it tightly in butcher paper or aluminum foil. Return it to the smoker.
5. When the brisket reaches an internal temperature of around 200°F, it is done. Place it on a large metal tray, then cover it with large, loose sheets of aluminum foil and a thick towel. (Or wrap it tightly in aluminum foil and place in a cooler at room temperature.)
6. Let the brisket rest for 30 minutes to an hour before carving.

SMOKEMASTER TIP: Close monitoring of the brisket's internal temperature will help you know when to adjust the smoker temperature, so the brisket is ready at the right time. The 225°F cooking temperature guide can be adjusted up or down by as much as 25°F without affecting the brisket. When the brisket reaches an internal temperature of between 155°F and 165°F, the cooking process will slow, often referred to as the stall. Refer to page 14 for more information on the stall.

RIB EYE STEAK WITH ROSEMARY-GARLIC BUTTER

PREP TIME: 20 minutes / **Cook time:** 45 minutes to 1 hour

There is nothing more gratifying than biting into a perfectly cooked rib eye steak. These steaks are cooked low and slow, then reverse seared to form a nice crust on the surface. Top with this rosemary-garlic compound butter and have a feast.

SERVES 4

SUGGESTED WOOD: Cherry, Apple, Oak

For the steaks

2 tablespoons olive oil
2 garlic cloves, minced
4 rib eye steaks
1 tablespoon sea salt
1 teaspoon freshly ground black pepper
½ teaspoon onion powder
½ teaspoon dried marjoram
¼ teaspoon smoked paprika

To make the steaks

1. Preheat the grill or smoker to 225°F. Depending on your cooker type, add your choice of wood chunks or smoke packet to the fire.
2. In a small bowl, combine the oil with the minced garlic. Brush both sides of the steaks with the mixture. In another small bowl, mix together the salt, black pepper, onion powder, dried marjoram, and smoked paprika. Season the steaks with this mixture and let them stand for 15 minutes.
3. Place the steaks on the smoker, close the lid, and cook for 45 minutes to 1 hour. Once the steaks reach an internal temperature of between 120°F and 125°F, remove from the smoker and increase the heat to 400°F. Place the steaks back in the smoker and sear for 2 to 3 minutes per side. (You can also set a cast-iron pan over direct heat for 5 minutes before placing the steaks in the pan to sear.)

For the compound butter

½ cup butter, softened but not melted
1 tablespoon finely chopped fresh rosemary
¼ teaspoon freshly ground black pepper
¼ teaspoon salt

To make the compound butter

4. In a medium bowl, combine the softened butter, rosemary, black pepper, and salt. Form it into a log shape on a 12-inch-wide piece of plastic wrap. Roll up the log in the plastic wrap and twist the ends to secure. Freeze for 30 to 40 minutes, then slice the log into ¼-inch-thick pats.
5. Once the steaks have seared, remove them from the smoker, and let them rest for 5 to 10 minutes. Top each with a pat of compound butter and serve.

SMOKEMASTER TIP: Not a fan of rosemary? Replace it with another fresh herb, like basil, oregano, or sage.

BEER AND ACHIOTE MARINATED FLANK STEAK

PREP TIME: 30 minutes, plus 12 to 24 hours to marinate / **Cook time:** 45 minutes to 1 hour

These super delicious flank steaks are perfect served as is or cut into strips to be used in tacos. They are marinated in a rich mixture of beer, chiles, and achiote paste, then smoked and reversed seared for a huge amount of flavor. See the SmokeMaster Tip following the recipe if you have trouble finding the guajillo peppers, chiles de árbol, or achiote paste.

SERVES 6 TO 8

SUGGESTED WOOD: Peach, Cherry, Oak

- 3 dried guajillo peppers
- 2 dried chiles de árbol, stemmed
- ½ cup lager beer
- 2 tablespoons white vinegar
- 2 tablespoons olive oil
- ½ yellow onion, roughly chopped
- 2 garlic cloves
- 2 teaspoons achiote paste
- 1 teaspoon salt
- ½ teaspoon cumin powder
- ¼ teaspoon freshly ground black pepper
- ¼ teaspoon dried oregano
- ¼ teaspoon cinnamon
- 2 (2½- to 3-pound) flank steaks

1. Submerge the guajillo peppers and the chiles de árbol in a small bowl of hot water and cover for 15 to 20 minutes to rehydrate.
2. Remove the peppers and chiles from the water and place them in a food processor with the beer, white vinegar, olive oil, chopped onion, garlic, achiote paste, salt, cumin, black pepper, oregano, and cinnamon. Puree the mixture, adding a few tablespoons of water if it's too thick. Taste and add more salt, if needed.
3. Place the steaks into a resealable plastic bag. Add the marinade and rub it into the steaks. Seal the bag and place into the refrigerator to marinate for 12 to 24 hours.
4. Preheat the grill or smoker to 225°F and remove the steaks from the marinade, discarding any excess. Depending on your cooker type, add your choice of wood chips or smoke packet to the fire.
5. Place the marinated steaks on the grates, close the lid, and cook for 45 minutes to 1 hour, or until your desired doneness.

6. Remove the steaks from the grill or smoker and increase the heat to 400°F. Place the steaks back into the smoker and sear each side for 3 minutes.
7. Remove and let the meat rest for 8 to 10 minutes before carving.

SMOKEMASTER TIP: If you are unable to find achiote paste, substitute with 1 teaspoon smoked paprika or 1 teaspoon achiote powder. Substitute dried guajillo chiles with New Mexico chiles or ground guajillo chili powder. A substitute for the chiles de árbol is a mixture of ½ teaspoon red pepper flakes and ¼ teaspoon cayenne pepper.

SMOKED AND BRAISED SHORT RIBS

PREP TIME: 25 minutes / **Cook time:** 4½ to 5½ hours

These smoked beef short ribs are braised in a wine and garlic mixture until they are fall-off-the-bone tender. This dish is incredibly versatile, too. Eat as is over pasta or rice, or remove the bones, chop up the meat, and make an incredible sandwich with your favorite toppings.

SERVES 4 TO 5

SUGGESTED WOOD: Oak, Cherry, Alder

For the ribs

- 2½ to 3 pounds beef short ribs
- 2 to 3 tablespoons vegetable oil
- 1½ tablespoons kosher salt
- 2 teaspoons freshly ground black pepper
- 1 teaspoon granulated garlic
- 1 teaspoon onion powder
- ½ cup apple cider vinegar
- ½ cup water

To make the ribs

1. Preheat the grill or smoker to 225°F and add desired wood chunks or smoke packet depending on your cooker type.
2. Remove excess fat from the tops of the ribs. Cut away the silver skin to expose the meat underneath, then brush lightly with vegetable oil. In a small bowl, combine the kosher salt, black pepper, granulated garlic, and onion powder. Season ribs liberally with the rub.
3. Place the ribs onto the grill or smoker, close the lid, and cook for 2½ to 3 hours. After the first hour, add the apple cider vinegar and water to a spray bottle and spritz the ribs every 30 to 40 minutes.

For the braising liquid

1 cup beef broth
¾ cup red wine (such as Merlot or Pinot Noir)
¼ cup unsalted butter, melted
2 teaspoons soy sauce
½ teaspoon salt
½ teaspoon freshly ground black pepper
2 garlic cloves

To make the braising liquid

4. In a medium bowl, combine the beef broth, wine, melted butter, soy sauce, salt, and pepper. Pour the mixture into a disposable aluminum pan large enough to fit all of the short ribs. Add the ribs to the pan with the mixture, then add the garlic cloves. Cover with foil and place the pan into the smoker to cook for 2 to 2½ hours, or until the internal temperature of the ribs reaches 205°F and they are very tender.

5. Remove from heat, unwrap, and let the ribs rest for 10 to 15 minutes before serving.

SMOKEMASTER TIP: Don't like red wine? Braise these short ribs with beer instead. We recommend a brown ale or lager.

SWEET AND SAVORY BEEF JERKY

PREP TIME: 25 minutes, plus 1 hour to marinate **/ Cook time:** 4 hours to 4½ hours

The smoker is one of the best tools for preparing homemade beef jerky. You can apply the right amount of smoke and end up with an incredible result versus using just a food dehydrator or your oven. With a sweet and salty marinade with a bit of a kick from the red pepper flakes, you'll want to make this beef jerky again and again.

SERVES 4

SUGGESTED WOOD: Oak

½ cup Worcestershire sauce
½ cup soy sauce
¼ cup brown sugar
2 to 3 garlic cloves, minced
2 teaspoons freshly ground black pepper
1 to 2 teaspoons red pepper flakes
1 teaspoon onion powder
1 pound top round steak

1. Combine the Worcestershire sauce, soy sauce, brown sugar, garlic, black pepper, red pepper flakes, and onion powder in a large bowl.
2. Trim all fat from the top round steak and cut into thin strips. Add the strips to the marinade mixture, cover, and refrigerate for 1 hour.
3. Preheat the grill or smoker to 150°F. Depending on your cooker type, add your choice of wood chips or smoke packet to the fire.
4. Remove the meat from the marinade and place it on a large piece of foil, spreading out the strips evenly. Discard the excess marinade.

5. Place the strips in the smoker and cook for about 3 hours, or until the surface takes on a deep brownish-black hue. Cover the strips loosely with foil. It's time to keep the smoke off but allow the moisture to escape. Return the meat to the smoker, close the lid, and cook for 1 to 1½ more hours. The meat should be well dried. (If you want it drier, continue to dry the beef jerky in a food dehydrator or your oven at a very low temperature.)
6. Let the jerky cool completely, then store in your fridge for up to 1 week, or place in vacuum-sealed bags and freeze for up to 6 months.

SMOKEMASTER TIP: Look for a lean cut of beef and remove all the surface fat. Adipose tissue carries moisture and can turn rancid quickly in dried form. So, the leaner the meat, the longer the shelf life of the jerky.

SMOKE & SEAR BURGER

PREP TIME: 15 minutes / **Cook time:** 1 hour 5 minutes

The classic method for searing meat is to start with a high temperature and then finish with a slower roasting temperature. However, smoke doesn't penetrate seared meat. So, for these burgers, we start with a low and slow smoke and then finish them off with a high-temperature reverse sear to get that crusted, caramelized surface on the patties.

SERVES 6

SUGGESTED WOOD: Maple, Cherry, Apple

3 pounds 85% lean ground beef
Pinch salt
Pinch freshly ground black pepper
2 medium onions
Olive oil, for brushing
6 slices cheese of choice
6 hamburger buns

1. Form the ground beef into 6 equal-size patties. Season with salt and pepper.
2. Preheat the grill or smoker to 225°F.
3. Place the burger patties on the cooking grate. Depending on your cooker type, add your choice of wood chunks or smoke packets as needed. Cook for 30 minutes.
4. Cut each of the onions into roughly inch-thick slices, brush with olive oil, and place them on the cooking grate next to the burger patties.
5. After 30 minutes of cook time, place a cast-iron griddle or pan on the grill or smoker to preheat.
6. Allow the patties and onions to smoke for an additional 30 minutes, or until the internal temperature of the patties reaches between 160°F and 165°F. Remove, cover, and keep warm.
7. Adjust the burners, vents, or pellet grill settings to increase your cooking temperature to between 400°F and 450°F and heat the cast iron to as high a heat as possible.

8. Place the patties in the pan and sear on each side for 1 to 2 minutes, or until they develop a deep color and crusty surface.
9. Remove the patties from the griddle and place on the buns. Top each patty with the smoked onions, a slice of cheese, and your favorite burger toppings.

SMOKEMASTER TIP: Coaxing a smoker or even many grills from a low and slow smoking temperature to a high searing temperature can take time. To take your burger patties (or anything cooked via the reverse-sear method) straight to high-temperature cooking, preheat a cast-iron skillet on your stovetop or use a grill side burner if you have one. You can sear right on your stovetop for speed and convenience.

SPICY SMOKY DINO RIBS

PREP TIME: 10 minutes / **Cook time:** 6 hours

If you've never had Dino Ribs, you're in for a treat. They are the big, meaty plate ribs from the first three bones of the cow's rib section. They are typically huge and, depending on the cut, they can be thick with meat and fat. Cooked fast, these ribs turn out tough and chewy. Smoked low and slow, however, they are tender and delicious.

SERVES 6 TO 8

SUGGESTED WOOD: Oak, Apple, Cherry

1 rack thick-cut beef plate ribs
⅓ cup kosher salt
¼ cup coarsely ground black pepper
1 tablespoon granulated garlic
1 tablespoon smoked paprika
2 teaspoons cayenne pepper (optional)

1. Trim away any loose bits of meat or fat from the ribs.
2. Preheat the grill or smoker to 225°F. Depending on your cooker type, add your choice of wood chunks or smoke packets to the fire. Plan for a 6-hour smoke time over indirect heat.
3. In a small bowl, combine the salt, pepper, granulated garlic, smoked paprika, and cayenne (if using). Season all sides of the ribs with the mixture.
4. Place the ribs on the grill or smoker, meat-side up, and smoke for 6 hours, or until the meat reaches an internal temperature of 195°F to 200°F.
5. Remove and cover with foil. Allow to rest for 15 minutes before carving and serving.

VARIATION: The traditional way for serving these beef ribs is without sauce. However, we recommend a sticky sweet or spicy tomato-based barbecue sauce, such as the Blood Orange BBQ Sauce (page 173) for this recipe. Brush the ribs with sauce 30 minutes before they are finished and let it cook in.

CHUCK ROAST BURNT ENDS

PREP TIME: 10 minutes, plus 20 minutes to rest / **Cook time:** 6 hours

This dish, also called "poor man's burnt ends," is a great substitute for traditional brisket burnt ends. Given the higher prices per pound for brisket, many people have begun gravitating toward economical cuts, like chuck roast. Done right, these little morsels of beef are amazingly delicious, and you won't miss the brisket at all. To give these burnt ends a different flavor profile with a tangy kick of citrus, skip the sauce in step 4 and toss them in the Blood Orange BBQ Sauce (page 173) in step 7.

SERVES 6 TO 8

SUGGESTED WOOD: Oak

- 1 chuck roast (about 4 pounds)
- 2 tablespoons coarse salt
- 4 teaspoons freshly ground black pepper, divided
- 1 tablespoon onion powder
- ½ teaspoon granulated garlic
- 1 tablespoon olive oil
- 1 small onion, finely chopped
- 2 garlic cloves, minced
- 1 cup ketchup
- ¼ cup brown sugar
- 1 tablespoon molasses
- 2 teaspoons chili powder
- ¼ teaspoon cayenne pepper

1. Trim any large chunks of fat from the chuck roast. In a small bowl, combine the salt, 3 teaspoons of black pepper, onion powder, and granulated garlic. Season the chuck roast evenly on all sides with the mixture.
2. Preheat the grill or smoker to between 250°F and 275°F, then place the roast on the cooking grates while adding wood chunks or smoke packets to the fire (depending on your cooker type). Cook for 3 hours.
3. After 3 hours, flip the chuck roast over, and continue cooking for another 2 hours.
4. While the chuck roast is cooking, heat the olive oil in a large saucepan over medium heat. Add the onion and cook for 2 to 3 minutes, until translucent. Add the garlic and cook for 1 minute. Stir in the ketchup, brown sugar, molasses, chili powder, remaining 1 teaspoon of black pepper, and cayenne. Simmer the barbecue sauce for 10 minutes, then remove from heat and set aside.

CONTINUED >

5. Once the roast reaches an internal temperature of between 190°F and 195°F, remove it from the smoker and wrap it in foil. Place in a warm place to rest for about 20 minutes.
6. Once rested, unwrap and chop into bite-size pieces.
7. Place the chopped chuck roast in a disposable aluminum pan or cast-iron skillet. Pour the barbecue sauce over the meat and toss to coat evenly.
8. Return to the smoker and cook for an additional 30 minutes. Serve.

VARIATION: Instead of adding the barbecue sauce, you can take this delicious smoked chuck roast, load it onto rolls, and serve with homemade au jus using beef broth or a beef base mix, for French dip sandwiches.

BERBERE SPICED SHORT RIBS

PREP TIME: 25 minutes / **Cook time:** 4½ to 6 hours

Berbere spice is a popular Ethiopian spice blend used in various foods, including stews, soups, and different meat dishes. We are using berbere spice as a barbecue rub for this recipe, and the flavor, combined with low and slow cooking, is exquisite.

SERVES 4

SUGGESTED WOOD: Oak, Cherry

- 2½ pounds thick-cut short ribs
- 2 teaspoons kosher salt
- 1 teaspoon paprika
- ½ teaspoon freshly ground black pepper
- ½ teaspoon cumin
- ¼ teaspoon cayenne pepper
- ¼ teaspoon granulated garlic
- ¼ teaspoon ground ginger
- ¼ teaspoon ground coriander
- ¼ teaspoon cinnamon
- ¼ teaspoon ground cloves
- 1 cup low-sodium beef broth, warmed

1. Preheat the grill or smoker to 225°F. Add desired wood chunks or chips during the first 2 hours of cook time.
2. Remove any excess fat from the tops of the ribs. Cut away the silver skin to expose the flesh beneath.
3. In a small bowl, combine the salt, paprika, black pepper, cumin, cayenne, granulated garlic, ginger, coriander, cinnamon, and cloves. Season the ribs liberally with the mixture.
4. Place the ribs into the grill or smoker, close the lid, and cook for 4½ to 6 hours, or until they reach an internal temperature of 210°F.
5. After the first hour, begin spritzing the ribs with the warmed beef broth every 30 minutes until done.
6. Once cooked, remove and place on a cutting board. Tent with foil, rest for 20 minutes, and serve.

SMOKEMASTER TIP: For the spritzing, you can substitute the beef broth with apple juice or a mixture of equal parts apple cider vinegar and water.

OSSO BUCCO

PREP TIME: 20 minutes / **Cook time:** 3½ hours

This Italian-inspired braised dish is traditionally made with veal shanks, but we've decided to mix two traditions for one flavorful outcome. Slow-smoked oxtail is a culinary tradition in the American South and work perfectly with this delicate, smoky osso bucco braising sauce.

SERVES 4 TO 5

SUGGESTED WOOD:
Oak, Alder

4 pounds beef oxtail, about 6 large pieces
Pinch salt, plus 1¼ teaspoons
Pinch freshly ground black pepper, plus ½ teaspoon
Pinch onion powder
1 to 2 tablespoons olive oil
1 small white onion, diced
2 garlic cloves, minced
3 medium carrots, peeled and chopped
1½ tablespoons tomato paste
¼ cup dry white wine
1 (14.5-ounce) can diced tomatoes
1 cup beef broth
1 tablespoon balsamic vinegar

CONTINUED >

1. Preheat the grill or smoker to 250°F. Depending on your cooker type, add a small amount of wood chunks or chips once the cooker is up to temperature. Do not add more wood after this.
2. Trim some of the excess fat from the oxtail, not removing all of it. Season with a pinch of salt, a pinch of black pepper, and onion powder on both sides. Place into the grill or smoker, close the lid, and cook for 1 hour.
3. Meanwhile, make the braising liquid by heating the olive oil in a large saucepan over medium heat. Add the onion and cook for 1 to 2 minutes. Then add the garlic and carrots and cook for 1 minute. Stir in the tomato paste, increase the heat to high, and deglaze the pan (scrape the browned bits off) with the wine. Add the diced tomatoes, beef broth, balsamic vinegar, remaining 1¼ teaspoons of salt, remaining ½ teaspoon of pepper, oregano, basil, and thyme. Let the sauce simmer for 1 to 2 minutes, then remove from heat.
4. Transfer the oxtail to a cast-iron Dutch oven or disposable aluminum pan. Pour the braising liquid over them.

½ teaspoon dried oregano
¼ teaspoon dried basil
¼ teaspoon dried thyme

5. Increase the heat of your grill or smoker to 275°F. Place the oxtail back in, uncovered, and cook for 1½ hours. Add more broth if needed. Then, cover the pot with a lid or pan with aluminum foil, and continue cooking for another hour, until fork-tender.
6. Remove from heat and let stand 10 minutes, uncovered. Skim away excess fat that has accumulated at the top. Serve as is or with mashed potatoes or polenta.

SMOKEMASTER TIP: If you'd like a more refined sauce, after removing the cooked oxtail from the braising liquid, place the meat in a large serving dish and cover with foil to keep warm. Remove excess fat from the liquid and discard. Pour the braising liquid into a blender and puree to a smooth consistency. Pour mixture over the oxtail, and garnish with chopped parsley.

KANSAS CITY BRISKET

PREP TIME: 10 minutes / **Cook time:** 10 hours

While brisket might be the barbecue of Texas, Kansas City is one of barbecue's greatest capitals. The Kansas City version of barbecue brisket has a shorter smoke time and a much sweeter rub and sauce. In Texas, it is about the meat. In Kansas City, it is about that barbecue flavor. To change up the recipe, replace the dry ingredients in step 3 with 1 cup of the Beef and Game Rub on page 167 (you'll need to double the rub recipe).

SERVES 6 TO 8

SUGGESTED WOOD: Oak, Apple, Cherry

For the brisket

1 (12- to 14-pound) brisket, untrimmed
¼ cup kosher salt
¼ cup brown sugar
2 tablespoons chili powder
2 tablespoons dry mustard
2 tablespoons paprika, not smoked
2 tablespoons granulated garlic
2 tablespoons onion powder
1 tablespoon freshly ground black pepper
2 teaspoons white pepper
2 teaspoons cayenne pepper
1 cup apple juice

To make the brisket

1. Pat the brisket dry with paper towels. Using a sharp knife, square the thinnest part of the brisket. The meat portion should be at least 1 inch thick.
2. Remove any large sections of fat, including any membrane. (The moisture of a smoked brisket comes from the fat between the muscle fibers and not the large fat cap on top. This excess fat slows the cooking process.)
3. In a small bowl, combine the salt, brown sugar, chili powder, dry mustard, paprika, granulated garlic, onion powder, black pepper, white pepper, and cayenne. Apply evenly over the entire surface of the brisket. Focus most of the seasoning on the meatier portions. Set the brisket aside while preparing your grill or smoker (about 30 to 45 minutes).
4. Preheat the smoker or grill. Prepare for a 10-hour cook time at a temperature of 225°F to 250°F. If you are using a grill or other cooker, make sure that the heat is indirect.
5. Place the brisket on the smoker, add any desired wood chunks or smoke packets, close the lid, and cook for about 6 hours.

For the sauce

1 cup ketchup
¼ cup brown sugar
¼ cup apple cider vinegar
¼ cup water
1 tablespoon paprika
1 tablespoon chili powder
1 tablespoon molasses
1 teaspoon cayenne pepper (optional)
½ teaspoon granulated garlic
¼ teaspoon salt
1 tablespoon butter

6. Once the brisket has reached an internal temperature of around 160°F (about 6 hours), lightly spritz the brisket with apple juice to keep the surface wet in appearance. Repeat every 45 minutes as needed.
7. When the brisket reaches an internal temperature of around 200°F, it is done. Remove and place on a large metal tray. Cover with loose sheets of aluminum foil and a thick towel, or wrap tightly in aluminum foil and place in a room-temperature cooler.
8. Let the brisket rest for 30 minutes to an hour before carving.

To make the sauce

9. In a medium saucepan over low heat, combine the ketchup, brown sugar, vinegar, water, paprika, chili powder, molasses, cayenne (if using), granulated garlic, and salt. Simmer for 15 to 20 minutes, stirring occasionally. Then remove from the heat, stir in the butter, cover, and set aside. Once the brisket has finished resting, carve and serve with the sauce as is or on thick slices of white bread.

SMOKEMASTER TIP: In Kansas City, burnt ends are a delicacy. To make them, once the brisket is cooked, cut away the point. This is the thicker, fattier portion that sits on the back, top portion of the brisket. Return this to the smoker and cook for 1 to 2 more hours. Chop into bite-size pieces and serve with a thick helping of the barbecue sauce.

SMOKED ROAST BEEF

PREP TIME: 10 minutes / **Cook time:** 3 hours

Using your smoker for this recipe not only produces a flavorful beef roast but keeps this eye of round moist and tender. We recommend pulling it off the smoker at a temperature of 140°F and letting the carryover heat bring the roast to 145°F.

SERVES 6 TO 8

SUGGESTED WOOD: Oak, Alder, Cherry

1 (4-pound) eye-of-round roast
1 tablespoon olive oil
4 tablespoons Beef and Game Rub (page 167)
⅔ cup low-sodium beef broth, warmed

1. Preheat the grill or smoker to 250°F. Depending on your cooker type, add your wood preference right before placing the roast on the smoker.
2. Rub the roast all over with the olive oil. Season the roast liberally with the Beef and Game Rub.
3. Place the roast in the smoker, close the lid, and cook for 3 hours, or until the internal temperature reaches 140°F.
4. After the first hour of cook time, spritz the roast with the warmed beef broth every 30 minutes for the remaining 2 hours.
5. Once cooked, remove and tent the roast with aluminum foil and let rest for 20 minutes. Uncover, slice, and serve.

SMOKEMASTER TIP: The thinner the slices, the more tender the roast will be. If you have a meat slicer, use that. Otherwise, use a very sharp knife and have a little patience. Keep the meat as moist as possible with small amounts of hot beef broth until you serve.

GARLIC LOVER'S PRIME RIB

PREP TIME: 20 minutes / **Cook time:** 4 hours

A tender and delicious prime rib roast prepared right in your smoker, this garlic and herb–crusted prime rib makes the perfect meal to serve during the holidays or on any special occasion.

SERVES 8 TO 10

SUGGESTED WOOD: Maple, Apple, Cherry

1 (6-pound) prime rib roast
1 tablespoon olive oil
8 garlic cloves, minced
1 tablespoon finely minced shallots
2 tablespoons butter, softened
2½ tablespoons Dijon mustard
2 tablespoons coarse salt
1 tablespoon finely chopped fresh rosemary
1 tablespoon finely chopped fresh marjoram
1 tablespoon coarsely ground black pepper

1. Trim any loose pieces of fat or meat from the roast.
2. Heat the olive oil in a small skillet over low heat. Add the garlic and shallots. Sauté for 2 minutes or until slightly translucent, then remove from heat.
3. In a medium bowl, combine the softened butter, Dijon mustard, salt, rosemary, marjoram, and black pepper to make a paste. Add the garlic and shallots and stir to combine.
4. Coat the roast evenly with the seasoning rub.
5. Preheat the grill or smoker to 250°F and plan for a 5-hour smoking time. Depending on your cooker type, add any desired wood chunks or smoker packets. Place the roast on the cooking grate and cook over indirect heat with the lid closed for 2 hours.
6. After 2 hours, rotate the roast for even cooking and continue smoking for another 2 hours, or until the prime rib reaches an internal temperature of 120°F to 125°F (medium-rare). Remove, tent with foil, and let rest for 20 to 30 minutes before carving.

SMOKEMASTER TIP: To get a crustier surface on the rib roast, preheat your oven to 450°F. Take the prime rib straight from the smoker and place it in a roasting pan in the oven. Then turn off the oven and cook the prime rib in the residual heat for an additional 15 minutes. Remove, rest, carve, and serve.

LEMON-OREGANO LEG OF LAMB

PREP TIME: 25 minutes, plus 4 hours to marinate / **Cook time:** 2½ to 3 hours

Seasoned with lemon, oregano, and garlic, this perfectly crusted, smoke-kissed lamb will tantalize your taste buds. This dish is perfect for the holidays and special occasions.

SERVES 6 TO 8

SUGGESTED WOOD:
Mesquite, Hickory, Oak

Zest and juice of 2 lemons
2 tablespoons olive oil
4 garlic cloves, minced
1 medium shallot, minced
¼ cup finely chopped fresh oregano
2 teaspoons finely chopped fresh thyme
2 teaspoons salt
1½ teaspoons freshly ground black pepper
1 (4-pound) boneless leg of lamb

1. In a nonreactive bowl, combine the lemon zest, lemon juice, olive oil, garlic, shallot, oregano, thyme, salt, and black pepper. Set aside.
2. Remove any large clumps of fat and silver skin from the surface of the lamb. Pat the entire leg dry. Unroll the lamb leg to expose the inner portion. Brush with some of the lemon-oregano mixture, then turn it over and brush the rest of the mixture on the outer part. Reroll the lamb and place into a glass baking dish. Cover tightly with plastic wrap and marinate in the refrigerator for 4 hours.
3. Preheat the grill or smoker to 250°F. Depending on your cooker type, add your choice of wood chunks or smoke packet to the fire.
4. While the smoker is preheating, remove the lamb leg from the refrigerator, uncover, and secure the roll with kitchen twine. Let stand at room temperature for 30 minutes.

5. Place the lamb into the smoker, close the lid, and cook for 2½ to 3 hours, or until the lamb reaches an internal temperature of between 135°F and 140°F (medium-rare to medium).

6. Remove the lamb from the smoker, tent with aluminum foil, and let rest for 10 minutes. Remove the twine, cut the lamb into ½-inch-thick slices, and serve.

SMOKEMASTER TIP: When tying a roast, start in the center and work outward toward the ends to ensure that it is secure and even.

HERB-CRUSTED RACK OF LAMB

PREP TIME: 25 minutes / **Cook time:** 1½ hours

This smoked rack of lamb is insanely delicious. The simple combination of garlic, fresh herbs, and smoke is the perfect complement to the natural flavor of the lamb. For a different flavor profile (or if you have some extra time), marinate the rack of lamb with the All-Purpose Marinade (page 168) in a large, sealed container and refrigerate for 12 to 24 hours before smoking. After the lamb has been marinated, follow the recipe as directed but skip step 3.

SERVES 6

SUGGESTED WOOD:
Apple, Oak

- 2 (2-pound) racks of lamb
- ¼ cup unsalted butter, softened
- 3 tablespoons Dijon mustard
- 2 tablespoons red wine vinegar
- 4 garlic cloves, minced
- 2½ teaspoons kosher salt
- 2 teaspoons Worcestershire sauce
- 2 teaspoons finely chopped fresh rosemary
- 2 teaspoons finely chopped fresh thyme
- 2 teaspoons finely chopped fresh marjoram
- ½ teaspoon freshly ground black pepper

1. Prepare your grill or smoker and preheat to 225°F. Depending on your cooker type, add your choice of wood chips or smoke packet to the fire.
2. Remove any large clumps of fat and silver skin from the rack of lamb.
3. In a medium bowl, combine the softened butter, Dijon mustard, red wine vinegar, garlic, salt, Worcestershire sauce, rosemary, thyme, marjoram, and black pepper. Apply this mixture onto the meat of the racks, avoiding the bones.
4. Place the racks into the smoker, bone-side down, close the lid, and cook for 1 to 1½ hours, or until the internal temperature of the lamb reaches between 135°F and 145°F (medium to medium-well).
5. Remove from the smoker and let rest for 10 minutes before carving.

SMOKEMASTER TIP: Some people have an aversion to lamb fat. However, we don't recommend trimming all the fat from a rack of lamb before it goes on the grill or smoker. Remove some of the large band of fat above the chop section, but let the rest of the fat render in the cooker. You can trim off whatever is left after it has cooked, if desired.

HOISIN-SOY LAMB SHANKS

PREP TIME: 25 minutes / **Cook time:** 3 hours 45 minutes to 4 hours 45 minutes

Smoked lamb shanks are amazingly tender and delicious. This recipe calls for lamb to be braised in a hoisin-soy marinade. Hoisin sauce has plenty of natural smokiness, so we recommend halting the smoking process when braising to avoid an overpowering smoke flavor.

SERVES 4

SUGGESTED WOOD: Oak

2 (2-pound) lamb shanks
½ teaspoon salt
½ teaspoon freshly ground black pepper
¾ cup hoisin sauce
¾ cup beef broth
¼ cup freshly squeezed orange juice
2 tablespoons brown sugar
1 teaspoon freshly squeezed lemon juice
2 garlic cloves, minced
2 teaspoons grated ginger
1 tablespoon tomato paste
¼ teaspoon white pepper
¼ teaspoon cinnamon
¼ teaspoon red pepper flakes

1. Preheat the grill or smoker to 250°F. Depending on your cooker type, add a small amount of wood chunks or chips.
2. Blot the lamb shanks with paper towels. Using a sharp knife, remove the silver skin around the shank and season with the salt and pepper.
3. Place the shanks into the grill or smoker, close the lid, and cook for 1½ to 2 hours, or until they reach an internal temperature of 165°F. Remove and place onto a cutting board.
4. Increase the heat of the grill or smoker to 325°F.
5. Combine the hoisin sauce, beef broth, orange juice, brown sugar, lemon juice, garlic, ginger, tomato paste, white pepper, cinnamon, and red pepper flakes in a medium bowl.
6. Place the shanks in a 9-inch-by-9-inch disposable aluminum pan or cast-iron pot. Pour the braising liquid over them and then place the pan or pot back into the cooker, uncovered, for 45 minutes. Add more beef broth if needed.

CONTINUED >

7. Cover the pan with aluminum foil (or place a lid on the pot) and cook for an additional 1½ to 2 hours, or until the lamb reaches an internal temperature of 200°F to 205°F.
8. Remove the lamb shanks from the smoker and uncover. Let stand for 10 to 15 minutes.
9. Shred the meat and place it back into the braising liquid, mixing to combine. Serve with your favorite side dish (see chapter 6 for ideas) or in tacos with sliced chile peppers and pickled vegetables.

SMOKEMASTER TIP: You can't overcook these lamb shanks, but you can dry them out. What you want is tenderness and flavor. Once the meat has had a chance to pick up a nice smoke flavor, you can add the braising liquid, cover, and let it cook for a few more hours. Not keen on too much smoke flavor? Complete the braising process in your oven at 325°F, starting with step 6. Need a substitute for hoisin sauce? Use a mixture of ¾ cup oyster sauce, ¼ teaspoon Chinese five-spice powder, and 1 tablespoon brown sugar.

VENISON STEAKS WITH BLACKBERRY-PORT SAUCE

PREP TIME: 20 minutes / **Cook time:** 1 to 1½ hours

These smoked venison steaks take on a unique flavor with the blackberry-port sauce. Bear in mind that this type of meat is quite lean, so we recommend cooking the chops to a medium-rare temperature. The addition of the blackberry-port sauce pulls the flavors and textures together beautifully. If you can't find ancho chile powder, feel free to use regular chili powder. Or, to simplify the process and change up the flavor profile of these venison steaks, replace the dry ingredients in step 2 with 3 teaspoons of the Beef and Game Rub (page 167).

SERVES 4

SUGGESTED WOOD: Apple, Oak, Alder

- 4 (7- to 8-ounce) venison steaks
- 1½ tablespoons vegetable oil
- 1¼ teaspoons kosher salt, plus ⅛ teaspoon
- 1⅛ teaspoons freshly ground black pepper, divided
- 1 teaspoon ancho chile powder

CONTINUED >

1. Preheat the grill or smoker to 225°F. Depending on your cooker type, add your choice of wood chips or smoke packet to the fire.
2. Brush the steaks on both sides with vegetable oil. In a small bowl, combine 1¼ teaspoons of salt, 1 teaspoon of black pepper, and the chile powder and rub the mixture into both sides of the steaks.
3. Place the steaks into the smoker, close the lid, and cook for 1 to 1½ hours, or until the internal temperature reaches 140°F to 145°F.

CONTINUED >

VENISON STEAKS WITH BLACKBERRY-PORT SAUCE CONTINUED

- 5 tablespoons unsalted butter, divided
- 1 medium shallot, minced
- 2 cups fresh blackberries, plus more for garnish
- ½ teaspoon balsamic vinegar
- 1 cup port wine
- 1 cup vegetable stock
- ⅛ teaspoon allspice

4. Meanwhile, melt 3 tablespoons of butter in a medium skillet over medium heat, then add the shallot and cook for 2 minutes. Add the blackberries, balsamic vinegar, and port wine, then increase the heat to high and bring the mixture to a boil. Once boiling, reduce the heat to medium-high and simmer until the liquid has reduced by 70 percent. Add the vegetable stock, allspice, remaining ⅛ teaspoon of salt, and remaining ⅛ teaspoon of pepper, and continue simmering until sauce has thickened to a syrup-like consistency. Add the remaining 2 tablespoons of butter and stir through.
5. Strain the sauce through a sieve to remove the blackberry seeds. Return to the pan, cover, and keep warm.
6. Once the venison steaks are done, remove them from the smoker and let rest for 10 minutes. Top with the sauce, garnish with a few fresh blackberries, and serve.

SMOKEMASTER TIP: Whenever you add a sauce to a smoked or grilled item, make sure the sauce is as hot or slightly hotter than the meat it is being added to. This will allow it to marry well with the meat and neither cook nor cool the dish.

VENISON LOIN ROAST

PREP TIME: 20 minutes, plus 6 to 12 hours to marinate **/ Cook time:** 1½ to 2 hours

This loin roast is steeped in a Hawaiian-inspired pineapple marinade and then smoked to perfection. As it's a lean cut, monitor this loin roast carefully and pull it off the smoker when its internal temperature is five degrees below your desired doneness.

SERVES 4

SUGGESTED WOOD:
Cherry, Apple

1 (1- to 1½-pound) venison loin roast
½ cup pineapple juice
2 tablespoons dark rum
2½ tablespoons soy sauce
1 tablespoon vegetable oil
1½ teaspoons grated fresh ginger
4 garlic cloves, minced
1 to 2 teaspoons chili sauce (such as sambal oelek or sriracha)
¼ teaspoon white pepper
½ teaspoon salt

1. Place the venison loin in a resealable plastic bag. In a medium bowl, combine the pineapple juice, rum, soy sauce, vegetable oil, ginger, garlic, chili sauce, and white pepper. Pour the marinade over the venison and work it into the meat. Seal the bag and place in the refrigerator for 6 to 12 hours.
2. Preheat the smoker to 225°F. Use wood chips for the first 40 minutes and stop for the remaining cooking time.
3. Remove the loin from the refrigerator and discard the excess marinade. Season the loin with the salt, and place into the smoker. Close the lid and cook for 1½ to 2 hours, or until the internal temperature is five degrees away from your desired doneness.
4. Promptly remove the loin from the smoker and let it rest for 10 minutes. Slice and serve.

SMOKEMASTER TIP: There is an old cooking tip that says to boil used marinades to make them safe to eat. This is not, however, the best solution. Many marinades, like the one in this recipe, would make a good sauce. The problem is that after sitting with the meat for several hours, the flavor of the marinade has changed. If you want to serve this venison loin roast with a sauce, make a double batch of the marinade. Use half to marinate the meat, and slowly simmer the other half until it thickens into a nice sauce for serving.

PORK

BEGINNER'S PORK BUTT

PREP TIME: 25 minutes / **Cook time:** 7 to 8 hours

Pork butt is a staple meat for barbecue. We call this recipe Beginner's Pork Butt, but that's just because it's so easy to execute. It's definitely not short on flavor—sweet and savory from the brown sugar and mustard, with a little kick of heat from the paprika and cayenne, this pork butt is a winning recipe.

SERVES 8 TO 12

SUGGESTED WOOD:
Oak, Hickory

1 (6- to 8-pound) pork butt
¼ cup yellow mustard
¼ cup dark brown sugar
¼ cup paprika
2½ tablespoons kosher salt
2 tablespoons freshly ground black pepper
2 teaspoons mustard powder
1½ teaspoons cayenne pepper
1 cup apple juice

SMOKEMASTER TIP: If you don't like the flavor of mustard, don't worry. Coating the pork butt with mustard will not impart a mustard flavor once the pork butt is cooked. Rather, it will help produce a great bark on the surface of the pork while keeping the spice rub in place.

1. Prepare the grill or smoker for an 8-hour cook time at 250°F. Depending on your cooker type, add your choice of wood chunks or smoke packet to the fire.
2. Remove any loose pieces of fat or hanging meat from the pork butt, but leave the rest of the fat intact.
3. Slather the pork with the yellow mustard on all sides. In a small bowl, combine the brown sugar, paprika, salt, pepper, mustard powder, and cayenne. Season the entire surface area of the pork with the mixture.
4. Place the pork butt into the smoker with the fattier side up. Add wood chunks or smoke packets to the fire during the first few hours of the smoke time. (This step isn't necessary if you're using a pellet grill or a hardwood smoker.)
5. Close the lid and cook the pork butt for 5 to 6 hours, until it reaches an internal temperature of about 160°F.
6. Remove the pork and place it into a large disposable aluminum pan. Pour the apple juice around the edges of the roast, then cover and seal the pan tightly with aluminum foil. Place the pan back into the smoker.

7. Continue to cook until the pork reaches an internal temperature of between 195°F and 205°F. Remove the pan from the smoker, leaving it covered, and place into an empty room-temperature cooler for 1 to 2 hours. If you do not have a cooler, wrap the pan with extra foil, cover tightly with 2 or 3 thick kitchen towels, and store in an unheated oven.
8. After the pork has rested for 1 to 2 hours, wearing heat-resistant gloves, peel back the foil and break apart the meat inside the pan with the cooking liquid. Serve as is or with your favorite barbecue sauce.

Chopped vs. Pulled

There is a reason pulled pork is called what it is. Tradition dictates that large cuts of pork, smoked to perfect tenderness, are pulled by hand into a pile of goodness. The process of pulling pork, also called a pig pickin', mixes the lighter and darker meats together while removing excess fat and any tough connective tissues.

Chopping smoked pork is just as delicious and can be an easier solution, especially if the meat hasn't achieved that ideal tenderness. To chop smoked pork, break it apart into large chunks. Remove any bits of fat and cut first against the grain and then again into small pieces. The goal of pulled or chopped pork is to create a pile of meat that fits loosely into a sandwich.

PORK BELLY BACON

PREP TIME: 20 minutes, plus 7 to 9 days to cure / **Cook time:** 2 hours

Making bacon from scratch is actually very easy. You need pork belly, brown sugar, kosher salt, and time. In fact, you need about a week. You start by curing raw, skinless pork belly in salt and sugar. Wrap it up tight in the refrigerator for 7 to 9 days. Then smoke the pork belly as low as you can go. You'll get delicious bacon every time.

SERVES 12

SUGGESTED WOOD:

Oak, Hickory

4 pounds pork belly, skin removed
1 cup brown sugar
¼ cup plus 2 tablespoons kosher salt (or other coarse, non-iodized salt)
2½ teaspoons coarsely ground black pepper
1 teaspoon curing salt (optional)

1. Trim away any loose pieces of meat or fat from the pork belly. It should be square and uniform in thickness. Pat it completely dry with paper towels.
2. In a medium bowl, combine the brown sugar, kosher salt, black pepper, and curing salt (if using). Mix well.
3. Coat the pork belly thickly with the mixture and place it into a large resealable bag. Refrigerate the pork for 7 to 9 days, turning it over once a day.
4. Preheat the smoker or grill to 200°F. Rinse the pork belly completely to remove excess salt and sugar. Pat dry with paper towels. Depending on your cooker type, add wood chunks or smoke packets to the smoker, then place the pork belly on the cooking grate.
5. Smoke for 2 hours, or until the internal temperature of the center of the pork belly reaches 150°F.
6. Remove from the smoker and wrap in butcher paper and then plastic wrap. Place immediately in the refrigerator to cool for at least 2 hours before slicing.

7. Before you are ready to slice the bacon, place it in the freezer for 20 minutes. This will make it easier to cut thin, even slices.

SMOKEMASTER TIP: There are many ways to add additional flavor to bacon. Once it has been rinsed and is ready to go on the smoker, try a thin layer of coarse black pepper to make peppery bacon. Or add finely chopped hot chiles to the curing mixture in step 2. Homemade bacon can be stored in the refrigerator for up to 7 days or in the freezer for up to 6 months.

COUNTRY-STYLE PORK RIBS

PREP TIME: 15 minutes / **Cook time:** 5 to 6 hours

Country-style pork ribs do not come from the rib section of the pig at all; rather, this cut comes from the pork shoulder region. These "ribs" are meaty and well marbled with fat, making them a great candidate for the smoker. To change up the flavor on these ribs, replace the dry rub in step 2 with the Pork Rib Marinade (page 170). Make one batch of the marinade, using half to marinate the ribs in step 2 and the other half to baste the ribs in step 7 instead of using the barbecue sauce mixture.

SERVES 6

SUGGESTED WOOD: Apple, Pecan, Hickory

- 3 pounds country-style pork ribs
- 2 tablespoons olive oil
- 2 tablespoons brown sugar
- 1 teaspoon onion powder
- 1 teaspoon salt
- 1 teaspoon freshly ground black pepper
- ½ teaspoon granulated garlic
- ½ teaspoon smoked paprika
- 1 medium yellow onion, thinly sliced

1. Preheat the grill or smoker to 225°F. Plan on a 6-hour cook time.
2. Cut away any loose pieces of meat or fat from the ribs. Blot dry with paper towels, then brush both sides with the olive oil.
3. In a small bowl, combine the brown sugar, onion powder, salt, pepper, granulated garlic, and smoked paprika. Season the ribs evenly with this mixture.
4. Place the ribs on the cooking grate. Depending on your cooker type, add wood chunks or smoking packets to the cooker. (This step is not necessary if you are using a pellet grill or a hardwood smoker.)
5. Close the lid and cook until the internal temperature of the ribs reaches 180°F.
6. Remove the ribs from the smoker and place them into an aluminum pan, then add the sliced onion. Increase the smoker heat to 250°F.

CONTINUED >

1¼ cups store-bought barbecue sauce
¾ cup apple juice
2 teaspoons apple cider vinegar
1 teaspoon Worcestershire sauce

7. In a medium bowl, combine the barbecue sauce, apple juice, apple cider vinegar, and Worcestershire sauce. Pour the mixture over the ribs, cover the pan with aluminum foil, and place it back into the smoker for another 2½ hours. Once the internal temperature of the ribs reaches between 200°F and 205°F, they are done. The ribs should be quite tender.
8. Remove the pan from the smoker and let sit for 20 minutes untouched. Then remove foil and serve.

SMOKEMASTER TIP: For a crispier crust, place the ribs over a direct fire once they have reached between 200°F and 205°F. Cook for about 4 minutes over high heat, turning frequently. Watch closely to make sure the barbecue sauce doesn't burn. For extra flavor, pour the juices from the pan over the ribs before serving.

MEMPHIS BABY BACK RIBS

PREP TIME: 15 minutes / **Cook time:** 5 to 5½ hours

Memphis is known for its "dry" ribs. These ribs start with a flavorful rub and are smoked low and slow. No sauce is added—just ribs, herbs, and spices. Smoked to perfection, these "dry" ribs will be anything but. To save some time, replace the dry ingredients in step 3 with ¼ to ½ cup of the All-Purpose Rub (page 165). Since the All-Purpose Rub can be used with so many different types of meat, it's a good idea to make a double or triple batch of it so you have it on hand for whatever you're smoking.

SERVES 4

SUGGESTED WOOD: Oak, Pecan, Hickory

2 racks baby back ribs
1 tablespoon paprika
1 tablespoon chili powder
2 teaspoons kosher salt
1 teaspoon granulated garlic
1 teaspoon onion powder
1 teaspoon white sugar
½ teaspoon ground cumin
½ teaspoon ground coriander
½ teaspoon dried oregano
½ teaspoon dry mustard
½ teaspoon cayenne pepper, adjust to preference
¼ teaspoon allspice
¼ teaspoon dried thyme
½ cup apple juice, room temperature
½ cup apple cider vinegar

1. Preheat the smoker or grill to 250°F with indirect heat.
2. Trim any excess fat and remove the membranes from the back of the ribs. Lightly blot them dry with paper towels. It's okay if a little moisture remains.
3. In a small bowl, combine the paprika, chili powder, salt, granulated garlic, onion powder, sugar, cumin, coriander, oregano, dry mustard, cayenne, allspice, and thyme. Divide the rub evenly between the rib racks. Season both sides but focus most of the rub on the meat side.
4. Place the rib racks into your smoker or grill, meat-side up. (Add any desired wood chunks or smoke packets to the cooker if you are using a charcoal or gas grill.)
5. Close the lid and let the ribs smoke for 1 hour.

6. In a spray bottle, combine the room-temperature apple juice and apple cider vinegar. After the first hour, lightly spritz the ribs. Do so every 30 minutes until the ribs register an internal temperature of 195°F and the meat is tender.
7. Remove the ribs, let them stand for 10 minutes, and slice for serving.

SMOKEMASTER TIP: To check the internal temperature of ribs, look for the space between the bones. The bones heat faster than the meat, so keep the point of your temperature probe away from them. Test the temperature of the ribs in multiple places. They don't always cook evenly, end to end. If you notice that one end of the rack is cooking faster, rotate the ribs in the grill or smoker.

KANSAS CITY BARBECUE SPARERIBS

PREP TIME: 15 minutes / **Cook time:** 6 hours

There is no arguing that the Kansas City Barbecue Spareribs have a distinctive quality all their own. These ribs are cooked low and slow, with just the right amount of smoke flavor, then slathered with a sweet, sticky tomato-based sauce.

SERVES 5 TO 6

SUGGESTED WOOD: Hickory, Oak, Mesquite

For the ribs

2 racks pork spareribs
¼ cup brown sugar
2 teaspoons paprika
2 teaspoons chili powder
1½ teaspoons sea salt
1 teaspoon freshly ground black pepper
1 teaspoon onion powder
1 teaspoon granulated garlic
½ teaspoon cayenne pepper
1 cup apple juice, divided

To make the ribs

1. Prepare the grill or smoker for a 6-hour, 225°F indirect cook. Add any wood chunks or smoke packets during the first 3 hours of the cooking time.
2. Blot the ribs dry with paper towels, remove the membrane from the back, and cut away any straggling pieces that might otherwise burn on the grill.
3. In a medium bowl, combine the brown sugar, paprika, chili powder, salt, pepper, onion powder, granulated garlic, and cayenne. Apply the rub to the ribs, front and back.
4. Place the ribs in the grill or smoker, meat-side up. Close the lid and cook, undisturbed, for 3 hours.
5. After 3 hours, remove the ribs from the grill or smoker and wrap each rack in aluminum foil with ½ cup of apple juice. Return to the grill or smoker and cook for 2 hours, wrapped.

For the barbecue sauce

1 tablespoon olive oil
2 garlic cloves, minced
1 cup ketchup
¼ cup water
¼ cup apple cider vinegar
⅓ cup brown sugar
1 tablespoon honey
1 tablespoon paprika
2 teaspoons chili powder
¼ teaspoon cayenne pepper
¼ teaspoon granulated garlic
Pinch salt
Pinch freshly ground black pepper
1 tablespoon unsalted butter

6. After the wrapped ribs have cooked for 2 hours, remove them from the grill and discard the foil. Return the ribs to the grill or smoker, meat-side up, and cook for 1 more hour. During the last 30 minutes of cook time, apply sauce every 10 minutes until the ribs reach an internal temperature of 195°F.

7. Carefully remove ribs from the grill or smoker, place them on a large cutting board, and let rest for 15 minutes.

To make the barbecue sauce

8. In a medium saucepan over medium-high heat, bring the olive oil, minced garlic, ketchup, water, apple cider vinegar, brown sugar, honey, paprika, chili powder, cayenne, granulated garlic, salt, and pepper to a simmer and cook for 1 minute. Reduce the heat to medium-low and simmer for 5 to 6 minutes, stirring often. Remove the pan from heat, add the butter, and stir until melted.

9. To serve, cut the racks into individual ribs and slather with the barbecue sauce.

SMOKEMASTER TIP: Wrapping ribs isn't necessary. The process described in this recipe is known as the 3-2-1 method. It is a great method for making tender, delicious ribs that are not too dry. Many experienced pitmasters, however, don't wrap their ribs. The key here is experience. Once you have mastered this recipe, try it without foil wrapping. You can also swap the foil for butcher paper.

PEACH NECTAR PORK ROAST

PREP TIME: 20 minutes / **Cook time:** 2 to 2½ hours

Pork loin is not known for being the most tender and moist cut of meat, but cooking it low and slow with a brown sugar rub and keeping it moist with peach nectar change the game. The peach nectar spritz will impart a light fruity flavor to the finished product. You can also use apple juice in place of the peach nectar.

SERVES 4 TO 5

SUGGESTED WOOD: Apple, Peach, Oak

1 (4-pound) pork loin roast
1½ tablespoons canola oil
1½ tablespoons brown sugar
2 teaspoons paprika
¾ teaspoon salt
½ teaspoon freshly ground black pepper
½ teaspoon onion powder
¼ teaspoon granulated garlic
½ teaspoon dried basil
⅓ cup peach nectar
2 tablespoons water

1. Prepare the grill or smoker for about a 2½-hour cook time at a smoking temperature of 225°F.
2. Trim the fat cap on the pork loin down to a ¼-inch thickness. Then score the meat diagonally, rotate it, and score again, creating a crosshatch pattern. Brush the entire roast with the canola oil.
3. In a small bowl, combine the brown sugar, paprika, salt, pepper, onion powder, granulated garlic, and basil. Apply the rub all over the roast.
4. Place it into the smoker, close the lid, and cook for 2 to 2½ hours.
5. After the first hour, combine the peach nectar with water in a spray bottle, and spritz the roast with it every 30 minutes. The roast is done once it reaches an internal temperature of 145°F.
6. Remove it from the smoker and let it rest for 10 to 12 minutes before slicing.

SMOKEMASTER TIP: Apply a peach glaze or fruit-based barbecue sauce during the last 40 minutes of cook time. Make sure that the cooking temperature stays below 265°F, which is the burning point of sugar.

TERIYAKI-GLAZED PORK TENDERLOIN

PREP TIME: 20 minutes / **Cook time:** 5 hours

This pork tenderloin is lightly seasoned, smoked, then slathered with teriyaki sauce. This allows the sauce time to caramelize on the surface of the pork, resulting in a beautifully glazed pork tenderloin.

SERVES 6

SUGGESTED WOOD:
Apple, Oak

- 1 (2½- to 3-pound) pork tenderloin
- 2 tablespoons olive oil
- 3 tablespoons brown sugar, divided
- 1 tablespoon paprika (not smoked)
- 3¼ teaspoons onion powder, divided
- 1 teaspoon salt
- ½ teaspoon white pepper
- 1 teaspoon garlic powder, divided
- ½ cup apple juice
- ½ cup soy sauce
- ½ cup water

CONTINUED >

1. Prepare the grill or smoker for a 5-hour cook time at 225°F.
2. Trim away any silver skin or hanging pieces of flesh and fat from the tenderloin. Blot dry with paper towels, and brush all over with olive oil.
3. In a small bowl, combine 2 tablespoons brown sugar, paprika, 2 teaspoons onion powder, salt, white pepper, and ½ teaspoon garlic powder. Season the tenderloin on all sides with the rub.
4. Place the tenderloin into the smoker or grill and cook for 1 hour. Depending on your cooker type, add any extra wood chunks or smoke packets. After an hour, pour the apple juice into a clean spray bottle and lightly spritz the pork with it.

CONTINUED >

⅓ cup white sugar
2 tablespoons Worcestershire sauce
1½ tablespoons white vinegar
1½ tablespoons vegetable oil
½ teaspoon grated fresh ginger

5. In a medium saucepan over medium-high heat, combine the soy sauce, water, white sugar, Worcestershire sauce, remaining 1 tablespoon of brown sugar, distilled white vinegar, vegetable oil, remaining 1¼ teaspoons of onion powder, remaining ½ teaspoon of garlic powder, and ginger to make the teriyaki glaze. Simmer for 1 minute, stirring often. Reduce heat to medium-low and let the sauce simmer for an additional 4 to 5 minutes. The sauce should reduce down to a syrup-like consistency, able to coat the back of a spoon. Remove from heat, cover, and keep warm.
6. Once the pork reaches an internal temperature of 130°F, it's time to apply the teriyaki glaze. Brush the tenderloin with it every 10 minutes until the internal temperature of the pork reaches 145°F.
7. Remove from the smoker and place onto a cutting board. Rest the tenderloin for 10 minutes, then slice and serve.

SMOKEMASTER TIP: If you'd like extra sauce for serving, double the teriyaki recipe and reserve half of it to drizzle on top of the sliced pork tenderloin. If the sauce is too runny for your liking, combine 1 teaspoon cornstarch with 1 tablespoon water, bring the reserved sauce to a simmer, add the cornstarch mixture, and stir well until the sauce thickens.

STEAKHOUSE PORK CHOPS

PREP TIME: 15 minutes, plus 4 to 6 hours to marinate / **Cook time:** 2 hours

These double-cut steakhouse pork chops are incredibly tender and flavorful. "Double cut" means the chops are made up of two stacked rib chop bones. Since they are thick, they benefit in both taste and texture from being marinated before hitting the smoker.

SERVES 2 TO 4

SUGGESTED WOOD: Apple, Peach, Cherry

1 cup pineapple juice
¼ cup soy sauce
4 garlic cloves, minced
2 tablespoons vegetable oil
2 tablespoons brown sugar
2 teaspoons grated fresh ginger
1 teaspoon Worcestershire sauce
1 teaspoon paprika
½ teaspoon white pepper
2 double-cut pork chops
Pinch salt
Pinch freshly ground black pepper

1. In a medium bowl, combine the pineapple juice, soy sauce, garlic, vegetable oil, brown sugar, ginger, Worcestershire sauce, paprika, and white pepper.
2. Place the pork chops in a large resealable plastic bag, pour in the marinade, and turn the chops to coat evenly, massaging them through the bag. Seal the bag and refrigerate for 4 to 6 hours.
3. Prepare the grill or smoker for a 2-hour cook time at 250°F. Depending on your cooker type, add your choice of wood chips or smoke packet to the fire.
4. Remove the pork chops from the marinade and lightly shake off any excess marinade. Season with the salt and black pepper.
5. Place the chops directly onto the cooking grates, close the lid, and cook for up to 2 hours, or until the internal temperature reaches 140°F.
6. Remove the pork chops and rest them for 10 minutes before serving.

SMOKEMASTER TIP: If you are interested in reverse searing, after smoking, move the chops over direct heat, and sear each side for 2 to 3 minutes. If you are working with a pellet cooker, remove the chops after cooking, increase the heat to 400°F, then return the chops to the cooker to sear for 2 to 3 minutes per side.

CURED AND SMOKED PORK SHANKS

PREP TIME: 15 minutes, plus 8 days to cure / **Cook time:** 2 to 3 hours

Smoked pork shanks or pork hocks are often overlooked when we think about barbecue. Brined and slow smoked, these tender shanks are delicious, especially when added to soups, beans, and stews. Pink curing salt, used to cure the pork shanks, is made up of sodium chloride and sodium nitrite. It's available online and in most grocery stores.

SERVES 4 TO 5

SUGGESTED WOOD:
Hickory, Apple

4 cups water
¾ cup salt
¾ cup dark brown sugar
2 teaspoons pink curing salt
5 pounds pork shanks

SMOKEMASTER TIP: Add flavor enhancers, like bay leaves, dried citrus peels, or whole peppercorns, to the brine solution. Once cooked, the pork shanks can be stored for up to 1 week in the refrigerator, or in the freezer in vacuum-sealed bags for 6 months.

1. In a large resealable plastic container, combine the water, salt, brown sugar, and curing salt. Stir and let it stand until the sugar and salt have dissolved, then stir again.
2. Submerge the pork shanks into the liquid, seal the container, and refrigerate for 1 week.
3. Remove the shanks from the liquid and rinse them under cold water. Place a wire rack on top of a baking sheet. Lightly blot the pork shanks dry, then place them on the wire rack. Refrigerate, uncovered, for 18 to 24 hours.
4. Prepare the grill or smoker for a 3-hour cook time at 200°F. Depending on your cooker type, add your choice of wood chunks or smoke packet to the fire.
5. Place the ham shanks directly onto the grill grates, close the lid, and slow smoke for 2 to 3 hours. Replenish the wood chunks or smoke packets throughout the cooking process to produce a strong smoke flavor.
6. Once the shanks have reached an internal temperature of 150°F, remove them from the smoker and let cool for 1 hour before using.

BRATWURSTS WITH SMOKED SAUERKRAUT

PREP TIME: 15 minutes / **Cook time:** 1 hour

For this recipe, both the bratwurst and the sauerkraut spend some time in the smoker. Although a simple recipe with just a few ingredients, the resulting flavor is incredible, and this is a delicious and easy way to feed a crowd.

SERVES 12

SUGGESTED WOOD: Apple, Peach, Oak

12 bratwurst sausages
3½ to 4 cups sauerkraut
4 cups vegetable broth
2 cups beer of choice
2 garlic cloves
12 hot dog buns

SMOKEMASTER TIP: You can substitute the beer with 1½ cups of apple juice and ½ cup of apple cider vinegar.

1. Preheat the smoker or grill to 225°F. Depending on your cooker type, add wood chunks or smoke packets.
2. Place the bratwursts into the smoker, close the lid, and smoke for 1 hour, or until they reach an internal temperature of between 160°F and 165°F.
3. Once the bratwursts have been on the smoker for 20 minutes, place the sauerkraut in an aluminum pan, and place the pan in the smoker for 30 minutes. Remove and let stand for 15 minutes before using. (If making the sauerkraut ahead of time, cool completely after cooking, cover the pan with foil, and store in the refrigerator.)
4. Meanwhile, in a large pot over medium-low heat, combine the vegetable broth, beer, and garlic and cook for 15 minutes. After 15 minutes, reduce to very low heat, or transfer broth mixture to a slow cooker and set temperature on warm.
5. Once the bratwursts have reached an internal temperature of between 160°F and 165°F, place them in the broth mixture until it is time to serve.
6. To serve, place a bratwurst into a hot dog bun and top with sauerkraut.

CAROLINA PULLED PORK

PREP TIME: 15 minutes, plus 30 minutes to dry brine **/ Cook time:** 8 to 10 hours

Pulled pork is the traditional barbecue dish of the Carolinas and one of the big three recipes in all of barbecue. It is, in fact, the original dish of barbecue. This low and slow cooking process can take up to 10 hours, but it's worth it. Good pulled pork relies on a sweet rub, exposure to smoke, and extra flavoring from a vinegar-based sauce. If you don't have dark chili powder, regular chili powder also works.

SERVES 6 TO 8

SUGGESTED WOOD: Apple, Oak, Pecan, Maple

For the pulled pork

1 (6- to 8-pound) pork butt
¼ cup brown sugar
1½ tablespoons kosher salt
1 tablespoon dry mustard
1 teaspoon dark chili powder
2 teaspoons freshly ground black pepper
1 teaspoon onion powder
1 teaspoon granulated garlic
½ cup apple juice, room temperature
2 tablespoons butter

To make the pulled pork

1. Prepare the grill or smoker for about a 10-hour cook time at 225°F. Depending on your cooker type, add your choice of wood chunks or smoke packet to the fire.
2. Trim down the thick layer of fat on the pork butt to about ¼ inch.
3. In a small bowl, combine the brown sugar, salt, dry mustard, chili powder, pepper, onion powder, and granulated garlic. Apply the rub to the entire surface area of the pork butt. Let stand at room temperature for at least 30 minutes.
4. Place the seasoned pork butt into the grill or smoker, close the lid, and cook until it reaches an internal temperature of about 160°F, 5 to 6 hours. Keep an eye on the smoker's temperature and adjust accordingly.

For the barbecue sauce

1½ cups apple cider vinegar
¼ cup white vinegar
2 tablespoons ketchup
1½ tablespoons brown sugar
1 tablespoon hot sauce (such as Tabasco)
1 teaspoon red pepper flakes
1 teaspoon salt
1 teaspoon freshly ground black pepper

5. Once it reaches 160°F, remove the pork and place in a large aluminum pan. Pour the apple juice around the edges of the roast, top with the butter, and seal tightly with aluminum foil. Place the pan back into the smoker for 3 to 4 hours, or until the pork reaches an internal temperature of between 195°F and 205°F. Remove the pan from the smoker but leave it covered. Place the pan into a clean, room-temperature cooler for 1 to 2 hours. If you do not have a cooler, wrap the pan with extra foil, cover tightly with 2 or 3 thick kitchen towels, and store in an unheated oven.

To make the barbecue sauce

6. Whisk together all ingredients for the barbecue sauce in a medium bowl and let it sit for 10 minutes until the sugar and salt have dissolved. Cover and set aside.

7. Wearing heat-resistant gloves, peel back the foil and break apart the meat inside the pan with the liquid. Lightly coat with the sauce and serve.

SMOKEMASTER TIP: Serve your Carolina Pulled Pork the traditional way, on white bread buns with a topping of tangy coleslaw. You can mix the barbecue sauce into the meat as you pull it, or serve it on the side as it is done in most Carolina barbecue joints. Serve with barbecue baked beans and a couple of pickle spears and you have the perfect meal.

PORK BELLY BURNT ENDS

PREP TIME: 15 minutes / **Cook time:** 5 hours

If you love brisket or chuck roast, aka poor man's burnt ends, then roll up your sleeves and get ready to enjoy this pork belly version. Keep in mind there's a reason that pork belly is so delicious—it is quite rich, so this dish makes a fantastic appetizer.

SERVES 8 TO 10

SUGGESTED WOOD: Pecan, Maple, Apple

- 1 (4-pound) slab pork belly, 1 to 1¼ inches thick, skin removed
- 4 tablespoons light brown sugar, divided
- 1 tablespoon kosher salt
- ½ tablespoon freshly ground black pepper
- 1½ teaspoons onion powder
- 1 teaspoon sweet paprika
- ½ teaspoon garlic powder
- ½ teaspoon chili powder
- ¼ teaspoon ground ginger
- ¼ teaspoon red pepper flakes
- 1 cup apple juice
- ½ cup Blood Orange BBQ Sauce (page 173), or store-bought
- 2 tablespoons cold butter, cut into small chunks

1. Preheat the grill or smoker to 250°F. Depending on your cooker type, have plenty of wood chunks or smoke packets ready. If the pork belly has more than ½ inch of fat, trim it down to that thickness. Otherwise, leave it alone.

2. In a small bowl, combine 2 tablespoons of brown sugar, salt, pepper, onion powder, paprika, garlic powder, chili powder, ginger, and red pepper flakes. Apply the rub evenly over the entire pork belly.

3. Place the pork on a wire rack, fat-side up, then place in the grill or smoker and cook for 1 hour.

4. Pour the apple juice into a spray bottle. After the pork has cooked for 1 hour, spritz it lightly with the apple juice. The surface should be slightly moist. Repeat spritzing as needed.

5. After about 4 hours of cooking, or when the pork belly reaches an internal temperature of 165°F, remove it from the smoker, wrap it in aluminum foil, and return it to the smoker. Cook until the internal temperature reaches 190°F, about 30 minutes.

6. Remove the pork belly, cut into 1-inch cubes, and arrange in a large aluminum pan in an even layer. Top with the Blood Orange BBQ sauce, the remaining 2 tablespoons of brown sugar, and the cold butter pieces.
7. Place the pan back into the smoker for 30 minutes, or until the sauce has caramelized. Remove and let stand for 15 minutes before serving.

SMOKEMASTER TIP: When buying pork belly, examine the edges. Look for a good strip of meat running all the way around the cut. Any section of the pork belly that is all fat top to bottom will not render during the smoke and will leave you with something you probably don't want to eat. The secret to great pork belly burnt ends is a chunk of meat sweetened by the rendering fat.

DOUBLE SMOKED HAM

PREP TIME: 20 minutes / **Cook time:** 4 hours

Why is it called double smoked? Because most hams are cold smoked and ready to eat right out of the package. The double smoke happens by hot smoking the already cold-smoked ham. This allows us to impart extra flavor and build a nice, candied crust on the surface.

SERVES 8 TO 10

SUGGESTED WOOD: Hickory

- 1 (6- to 7-pound) ham, unsliced and bone-in
- 2 tablespoons whole cloves, for studding
- 2½ cups root beer
- 1 cup packed dark brown sugar
- 2 tablespoons melted butter
- 1½ tablespoons Dijon mustard
- 1 tablespoon red wine vinegar
- 2 teaspoons grated fresh ginger

1. Preheat the grill or smoker to 225°F.
2. Set the ham on a large cutting board. Blot it dry with paper towels and stud the top surface with cloves, spacing them an inch apart in a diamond pattern.
3. Place the ham into the smoker. Depending on your cooker type, add wood chunks or smoke packets to the fire. Close the lid and smoke for 2 hours. Keep an eye on the temperature and adjust as needed.
4. In a medium bowl, combine the root beer, brown sugar, butter, Dijon mustard, red wine vinegar, and ginger. Cover and set aside until ready to use.
5. After 2 hours of cooking, brush the ham with the glaze. Repeat glazing every 30 to 40 minutes until the ham reaches an internal temperature of 140°F, about 2 hours.
6. Carefully remove the ham from the smoker and place it on a clean cutting board. Let it rest for 15 to 30 minutes, then carve and serve.

SMOKEMASTER TIP: The glaze used in this recipe has a good deal of sugar. If you take the glazed ham from the smoker and place it in a preheated 450°F oven, the sugar will caramelize. Once the ham is in the oven, turn off the heat and let the ham cook in the residual heat for 15 minutes. This will provide a crispy, sugary surface.

CENTRAL TEXAS PORK STEAKS

PREP TIME: 20 minutes / **Cook time:** 2½ to 3 hours

Pork steaks originate from the bone-in pork shoulder region, making this cut a prime candidate for low and slow cooking. Because of this, along with the fact that they are delicious, pork steaks continue to grow in popularity among barbecue enthusiasts.

SERVES 4

SUGGESTED WOOD: Hickory

½ cup brown sugar
2 tablespoons kosher salt
1 tablespoon chili powder
2 teaspoons freshly ground black pepper
1 teaspoon onion powder
4 (1-inch-thick) pork steaks
½ cup apple juice

1. Preheat the smoker or grill to 250°F.
2. In a small bowl, combine the brown sugar, salt, chili powder, pepper, and onion powder. Apply the rub liberally to both sides and edges of the pork steaks.
3. Place the pork steaks right on the grill grates. Depending on your cooker type, add wood chunks or smoke packets to the fire. Close the lid and cook for 1 hour.
4. Pour the apple juice into a spray bottle. After 1 hour of cooking, spritz the steaks with the apple juice. Continue to cook, spritzing every 30 minutes, until they reach an internal temperature of between 180°F and 185°F, about 1½ to 2 hours.
5. Remove the steaks, let them rest for 10 to 15 minutes, and serve.

SMOKEMASTER TIP: Try the Quick Brine (page 171) for a juicier pork steak. Submerge in the solution for 2 hours, then lightly rinse the pork steaks, blot dry with paper towels, season, and cook as directed.

OINK ROLLUPS

PREP TIME: 30 minutes / **Cook time:** 2 hours

These little treasures are one of our signature appetizer recipes. Three types of pork are used, including ground pork, bratwurst sausage, and of course, bacon. Use your favorite sweet rub to customize the flavor profile to your liking.

SERVES 9 TO 10

SUGGESTED WOOD: Apple, Oak, Cherry

1 pound ground pork
1 pound bratwurst sausage, casings removed
1 tablespoon brown sugar
1 teaspoon paprika
½ teaspoon chili powder
½ teaspoon onion powder
¼ teaspoon cayenne pepper
1 pound bacon
1 cup store-bought barbecue sauce

1. Preheat the grill or smoker to 250°F. Depending on your cooker type, add your choice of wood chunks or smoke packet to the fire.
2. Combine the ground pork, bratwurst sausage, brown sugar, paprika, chili powder, onion powder, and cayenne in a large bowl. Form the mixture into small rectangles about 1 inch thick and 2 inches long.
3. Cut the bacon strips in half lengthwise and separate them. Set a rectangle on one end of each strip of bacon and roll it up. Secure each rollup with a toothpick.
4. Place the rollups directly onto the grill grates, close the lid, and cook for 1 hour. Flip them and cook for another 30 minutes.
5. During the last 30 minutes of cook time, brush the rollups with barbecue sauce twice. Coat one side, then 15 minutes later, turn them over and brush with sauce on the other side. They are done once they reach an internal temperature of 175°F.

VARIATION TIP: Customize these rollups by adding diced jalapeños and ½ cup shredded jack cheese to the ground pork mixture.

APPLE BARBECUE RIBLETS

PREP TIME: 15 minutes / **Cook time:** 2 hours

These riblets are smoked low and slow, then slathered with a flavorful apple barbecue sauce. They make excellent appetizers but can also be served as the main protein for dinner. If you can't find apple jelly for the sauce or prefer a different flavor, feel free to use peach jelly instead.

SERVES 5

SUGGESTED WOOD: Apple

For the riblets

2½ pounds pork riblets
¼ cup Dijon mustard (use more if needed)
2 tablespoons plus 2 teaspoons All-Purpose Rub (page 165)

For the sauce

½ cup ketchup
½ cup apple jelly
¼ cup water
¼ cup apple cider vinegar
¼ cup dark brown sugar
1 teaspoon All-Purpose Rub
1 tablespoon blackstrap molasses
½ teaspoon Worcestershire sauce
1 tablespoon butter

To make the riblets

1. Preheat the grill or smoker to 250°F.
2. Coat each riblet section with Dijon mustard. Then season the riblets on both sides with the All-Purpose Rub.
3. Place the riblets into the smoker, close the lid, and cook for about 1 hour, or until the riblets reach an internal temperature of between 175°F and 180°F, before saucing. Add any desired wood chunks or smoke packets when you put the riblets on the smoker or grill.

To make the sauce

4. Meanwhile, in a small saucepan over medium-high heat, combine the ketchup, apple jelly, water, apple cider vinegar, brown sugar, and All-Purpose Rub and simmer for 1 minute. Reduce the heat to medium-low, and simmer for 5 minutes, stirring occasionally. Add the molasses and Worcestershire sauce, and simmer for 2 more minutes. Reduce the heat to low, if needed. Add the butter and stir until melted. Remove from heat, cover, and set aside.

CONTINUED >

5. After 1 hour of cooking, baste the riblets with the sauce every 15 minutes during the remaining hour of cook time.
6. Once the riblets reach an internal temperature of 195°F, they are done. Remove from the smoker, let them rest for about 10 minutes, and serve as is, or slice into individual riblets.

SMOKEMASTER TIP: Riblets are smaller pieces cut from a full rack of ribs. They are not to be confused with rib tips, which are meaty chunks from the underside of spareribs. Look for these inexpensive cuts at your local grocery store or ask your butcher to cut them for you.

PINOY PORK KEBABS

PREP TIME: 25 minutes, plus 6 to 10 hours to marinate / **Cook time:** 1½ to 2 hours

These Filipino-style pork kebabs are so easy to make and flavorful, too. Typically, this recipe includes banana ketchup, which tastes nothing like bananas but is a widely used condiment in Filipino cuisine. Our recipe calls for tomato ketchup, but if you have access to its counterpart, we say go for it.

SERVES 5

SUGGESTED WOOD: Apple, Oak, Maple

1 cup ketchup
½ cup soy sauce
½ cup lemon-lime soda
Juice of 1 lemon
2 garlic cloves, minced
2 tablespoons olive oil
1 tablespoon sriracha
1 tablespoon white sugar
1 teaspoon onion powder
½ teaspoon salt
½ teaspoon freshly ground black pepper
1 (3-pound) pork butt or pork tenderloin

SMOKEMASTER TIP: When grilling or smoking kebabs, keep the pork (or whatever meat you are using) spaced on the skewers. This reduces cooking time and allows smoke and heat to get to more of the meat's surface area.

1. In a large nonreactive bowl, combine the ketchup, soy sauce, soda, lemon juice, garlic, olive oil, sriracha, sugar, onion powder, salt, and black pepper. Reserve ¾ cup of the marinade for basting.
2. Trim away excess fat from the pork and cut it into 1¼-inch cubes. Place the pork into the bowl with the marinade and toss to coat. Cover the bowl tightly with plastic wrap, and refrigerate for 6 to 10 hours. If using wooden skewers, soak them in tepid water 30 minutes before using.
3. Preheat the grill or smoker to 250°F. Depending on your cooker type, add your choice of wood chunks or smoke packet to the fire.
4. Remove the pork from the refrigerator and discard the excess marinade. Thread the pork onto skewers, about 5 pieces per skewer.
5. Place the skewers into the smoker, close the lid, and cook for 1½ to 2 hours, turning the kebabs after 1 hour. During the last 30 minutes of cook time, baste the skewers with the reserved marinade.
6. Once the internal temperature of the kebabs reaches 155°F, remove from the smoker and let them rest for 10 minutes before serving.

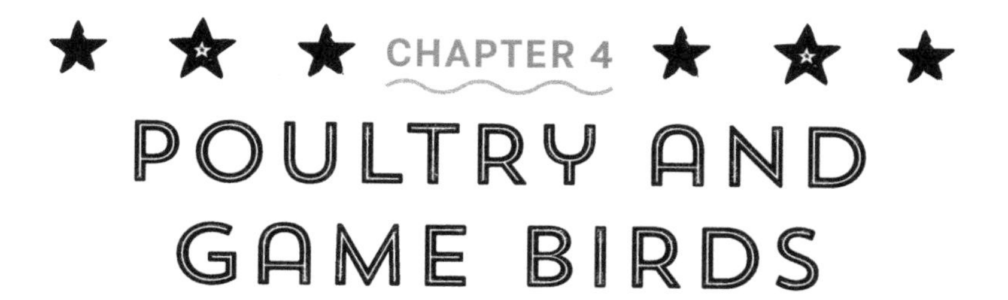

CHAPTER 4 POULTRY AND GAME BIRDS

BBQ WHOLE CHICKEN

PREP TIME: 20 minutes / **Cook time:** 3½ to 4 hours

This whole-chicken recipe is perfect for those just starting their smoked meat journey. All it requires is slow roasting in a smoky environment. There are two ways to serve this smoked chicken: carve it like a typical roasted chicken, or pull the meat as you would with pork and serve it on sandwiches. If you like, you can replace the dry ingredients in step 3 with ¼ cup of the Poultry Rub (page 166).

SERVES 8

SUGGESTED WOOD:
Cherry, Apple

- 2 (3½- to 4-pound) whole chickens
- 2 tablespoons vegetable oil
- ⅓ cup paprika
- ¼ cup chili powder
- 1 tablespoon salt
- 1 tablespoon onion powder
- 2 teaspoons ground cumin
- 2 teaspoons dry mustard
- 2 teaspoons granulated garlic
- 2 teaspoons freshly ground black pepper
- 2 teaspoons dried parsley
- 1 teaspoon dried thyme

1. Preheat the smoker or grill to 250°F.
2. Trim away any excess skin, blot chickens dry with paper towels, and brush them all over with vegetable oil.
3. Combine the paprika, chili powder, salt, onion powder, cumin, dry mustard, granulated garlic, black pepper, parsley, and thyme in a small bowl. Divide the mixture in half, and use one half to season each chicken. Massage the rub under the breast skin and inside the cavity as well.
4. Depending on your cooker type, add desired wood chips or chunks, if using, right before placing the chickens on to cook. Place chickens into the smoker or grill, close the lid, and cook for 3 to 4 hours, depending on the size and the equipment you're using. It takes roughly 45 minutes per pound to smoke a chicken. Once the chickens reach 195°F in the thigh area and 185°F in the breast area, they are done.

5. Remove the chickens from your grill or smoker and let them rest for 10 minutes before carving and serving. Use heat-resistant food-safe gloves if you are planning on pulling the chicken.

SMOKEMASTER TIP: Low and slow cooking tends to leave chicken skin with a thick, rubbery texture. To help mitigate this, during the last 30 to 40 minutes of cooking time, remove the chickens from the grill or smoker, cover, and keep warm. Increase the heat to 350°F, place the chickens back in, and finish cooking at this temperature. Whether you carve the chickens into slices or pull them to use on sandwiches, serve with the Alabama White Sauce (page 172) for an unbeatable combination.

PERUVIAN CHICKEN WITH AJI VERDE

PREP TIME: 20 minutes, plus 8 to 24 hours to marinate / **Cook time:** 3 to 4 hours

Peruvian chicken (*pollo a la brasa*) is a roasted chicken dish that originated in Peru during the 1950s. There is no argument that this famous South American chicken has garnered global appeal, and rightfully so. Typically, this dish is served alongside rice and vegetables, but it's satisfying enough to be served on its own.

SERVES 4 TO 5

SUGGESTED WOOD:
Apple, Oak

For the chicken

Juice of 2 limes
3 garlic cloves, minced
3 tablespoons olive oil
1 tablespoon white vinegar
1 tablespoon aji amarillo paste (see tip)
1 tablespoon aji panca paste (see tip)
1 tablespoon soy sauce
1½ teaspoons salt
2 teaspoons ground cumin
1½ teaspoons freshly ground black pepper
½ teaspoon smoked paprika
1 (3-pound) whole chicken

To make the chicken

1. Combine the lime juice, garlic, olive oil, white vinegar, aji amarillo paste, aji panca paste, soy sauce, salt, cumin, black pepper, and smoked paprika in a blender or food processor. Puree, then set aside.
2. Pat the chicken dry with paper towels. Trim away any loose skin. Rub the marinade all over the chicken, including under the breast skin and inside the cavity. Place into a glass baking dish and cover tightly with plastic wrap. Marinate in the refrigerator for 8 to 24 hours.
3. Preheat the grill or smoker to 250°F. Depending on your cooker type, add your desired smoke packets or wood chips to the fire before putting the chicken on to cook.

For the aji verde

1 cup chopped fresh cilantro
⅔ cup mayonnaise
1½ tablespoons freshly squeezed lime juice
1 tablespoon aji amarillo paste (see tip)
1 garlic clove
¼ teaspoon onion powder
¼ teaspoon salt

4. Place the marinated chicken into the smoker or grill, close the lid, and cook for 3 to 4 hours, or until the internal temperature of the thigh meat reaches 195°F. If you'd like some crispness on the skin, increase the heat of your cooker to 350°F and broil the chicken for the last 30 minutes of cook time.
5. Once cooked, remove, place on a clean cutting board, and loosely tent with aluminum foil. Let it rest for 10 to 15 minutes before carving.

To make the aji verde

6. Place the cilantro, mayonnaise, lime juice, aji amarillo paste, garlic, onion powder, and salt into a food processor or blender. Puree the mixture and serve with the carved chicken.

SMOKEMASTER TIP: If you cannot find aji amarillo paste, use 1 small, seeded jalapeño instead. For aji panca, 1 teaspoon of ancho chile powder makes a great substitute in a pinch. Aji panca is a little spicy, so factor that in accordingly.

SMOKED BEER-CAN CHICKEN

PREP TIME: 25 minutes **/ Cook time:** 1 to 1½ hours

This smoked version of the classic beer-can chicken takes the temperature down for low and slow cooking. You'll be surprised at how tender and moist this chicken will turn out.

SERVES 4 TO 5

SUGGESTED WOOD: Apple, Cherry, Oak

- 1 (3½- to 4-pound) whole chicken
- 1 tablespoon olive oil
- 2 tablespoons Poultry Rub (page 166)
- 1 (12-ounce) can lager beer
- 2 tablespoons chopped shallots
- 2 tablespoons red wine vinegar
- 3 garlic cloves, chopped
- ¼ onion, peeled but kept whole

1. Prepare the grill or smoker for a 350°F indirect cook. Add wood to the coals a few minutes before the chicken goes on.
2. Pat the chicken dry with paper towels, and trim away any excess skin. Brush all over with olive oil.
3. Season the chicken liberally with the Poultry Rub, making sure to get under the skin of the breast.
4. Pour half the beer into a glass, and enjoy. Using a can opener, carefully remove the round lip at the top of the can. Place the shallots, red wine vinegar, and garlic inside the can.
5. Place the chicken on a metal baking sheet or a large cutting board. Carefully insert the beer can about two-thirds of the way into the chicken cavity with the chicken standing up. Place the onion wedge into the neck opening to seal it up.
6. Transfer the chicken to the smoker or grill, close the lid, and cook for 1 to 1½ hours, or until the internal temperature reaches 175°F to 180°F in the thigh region.

7. Once cooked, use heat-resistant gloves to remove the chicken from the smoker. Take out the beer can and onion wedge and discard them. Place the chicken onto a clean cutting board and tent with aluminum foil to rest for 10 to 15 minutes. Carve and serve.

SMOKEMASTER TIP: Chicken is safe to eat at 165°F. However, at this temperature, dark meat areas, like the thigh and leg portions, will have a chewy texture. If you like that, by all means, remove it at 165°F. Collagen breakdown occurs past this point, so cooked thigh meat between 175°F and 180°F is optimal.

Tips to Not Fowl It Up

Chicken is one of the most forgiving meats you can smoke. All you need to do is make sure it reaches an internal temperature of 165°F for safe consumption. Chicken is typically a more affordable protein than beef or pork, and the breast section is incredibly versatile and yields delicious smoky morsels. Most recipes that call for chicken breast can benefit from a little smoky flavor.

We recommend a quick brine for chicken breasts. Combine 1 cup of water with 1 tablespoon each of salt and sugar per breast. The brining time can be as short as 1 hour or up to 4 hours. Remove the breasts from the brine, rinse in cold water, blot dry, and season to your liking. Placed in a grill or smoker at 250°F, these chicken breasts will be cooked in 45 minutes.

You can master your smoking skills, test out a new cooker, or prepare an easy and quick weeknight dinner using chicken breasts. Try adding a few breasts to the cooker next time you have space. They keep in the refrigerator for up to 5 days or can be frozen for future use. Smoked chicken breasts are great on a salad, in a sandwich, or in your favorite casseroles, soups, and stews–the possibilities are endless.

SMOKY SPATCHCOCK CHICKEN

PREP TIME: 25 minutes, plus 4 to 8 hours to marinate / **Cook time:** 3½ hours

To spatchcock a chicken means to remove the backbone and rib sections, then flatten it out. This shape helps the chicken cook faster and more evenly, with the breast and thigh meat finishing at the same time.

SERVES 4 TO 5

SUGGESTED WOOD: Cherry, Maple, Apple

1 (3-pound) whole chicken
1½ tablespoons olive oil
1 tablespoon freshly squeezed lime juice
1 tablespoon paprika
2 teaspoons chili powder
1 teaspoon onion powder
1 teaspoon white sugar
1 teaspoon granulated garlic
½ teaspoon freshly ground black pepper
½ teaspoon herbes de Provence
¼ teaspoon cayenne pepper

1. Place the chicken, breast-side down, onto a cutting board. Using a pair of kitchen shears, cut from the tail to the neck on either side of the backbone. Remove the backbone and discard. Trim away any protruding rib bones. Turn the chicken over, and press on the breast sections and thighs to flatten out the chicken.
2. In a small bowl, combine the olive oil, lime juice, paprika, chili powder, onion powder, sugar, granulated garlic, black pepper, herbes de Provence, and cayenne to form a paste. Rub the paste all over the chicken and apply some under the breast skin. Place the chicken into a large resealable container or freezer bag, and refrigerate for 4 to 8 hours.
3. Preheat the grill or smoker to 275°F. Depending on your cooker type, add your preferred wood chips.
4. Place the marinated chicken directly onto the grates, breast-side up. Flatten out the edges so that the chicken lies evenly. Close the lid and cook for 3 to 3½ hours, or until the breast and thigh meat register between 165°F and 175°F.
5. Remove from the smoker, tent loosely with aluminum foil, and rest for 10 minutes. Carve and serve.

SMOKEMASTER TIP: Smoky Spatchcock Chicken works well with Alabama White Sauce (page 172). Dip or drizzle on top of the chicken right before serving.

JALAPEÑO POPPER–STUFFED CHICKEN BREASTS

PREP TIME: 25 minutes / **Cook time:** 1½ hours

What could be better than a chicken breast stuffed with cheese and jalapeños, then wrapped in bacon and smoked? This is a decadent main course that will have your friends and family asking for more.

SERVES 4

SUGGESTED WOOD:
Cherry, Maple

- 4 large boneless, skinless chicken breasts
- 8 ounces cream cheese
- ⅓ cup seeded, diced jalapeños
- 3 medium scallions, finely chopped
- 1 cup shredded cheddar cheese
- ¼ teaspoon dried oregano
- ¼ teaspoon chili powder
- Pinch salt
- Pinch freshly ground black pepper
- 16 thin bacon slices

1. Preheat the grill or smoker to 250°F. Depending on your cooker type, add your wood of choice.
2. Trim off any knobs of fat on the surface of the chicken breasts. Make a 3- to 3½-inch-long incision in the side roughly halfway into each breast. Do not cut all the way through; you are simply creating a pocket to hold the filling.
3. In a medium bowl, combine the cream cheese, jalapeños, scallions, cheddar cheese, oregano, chili powder, salt, and pepper. Scoop ⅓ to ½ cup of filling into each breast and gently close. Wrap each breast with 4 slices of bacon and secure with toothpicks.
4. Place the chicken directly onto the grates, close the lid, and cook for 1½ hours, or until the internal temperature in the thickest part of the chicken reaches 165°F.
5. Carefully remove from your smoker or grill and plate. Serve each breast whole or cut in half and share.

SMOKEMASTER TIP: For a little added sweetness, mix ⅓ cup of your favorite bottled barbecue sauce with ⅓ cup real maple syrup. Once the chicken reaches an internal temperature of 155°F, baste the chicken breasts with it. Close the lid and continue cooking until the chicken reaches 165°F.

HOISIN CHICKEN THIGHS

PREP TIME: 25 minutes / **Cook time**: 2½ hours

Chicken thighs are great in the smoker or grill because they are moister than their white-meat counterparts. Serve these Hoisin Chicken Thighs alongside a bowl of the Pineapple Soy Glaze (page 174) for dipping.

SERVES 8

SUGGESTED WOOD:
Alder, Oak

- 8 bone-in, skin-on chicken thighs
- ¼ cup brown sugar, plus 1 tablespoon
- 2 tablespoons paprika
- 2¼ teaspoons onion powder, divided
- 1 teaspoon granulated garlic
- ½ teaspoon cayenne pepper
- ¼ teaspoon ground ginger
- 1 tablespoon vegetable oil
- 2 garlic cloves, minced
- ½ cup hoisin sauce
- ¼ cup ketchup
- 2 tablespoons dry sherry
- 1 tablespoon white vinegar
- 1 tablespoon water
- 2 teaspoons soy sauce
- ½ teaspoon sesame oil

1. Preheat the grill or smoker to 275°F. Depending on your cooker type, add your wood of choice.
2. Trim away excess skin from the chicken thighs, leaving enough on to cover the flesh.
3. In a small bowl, combine ¼ cup brown sugar, paprika, 2 teaspoons onion powder, granulated garlic, cayenne, and ginger. Season the thighs on both sides and under the skin.
4. Place the chicken into the grill or smoker, close the lid, and cook for 2½ hours, or until the internal temperature reaches 165°F.
5. In a small saucepan over medium heat, heat the vegetable oil. Add the garlic and cook for 30 seconds. Add the hoisin sauce, ketchup, sherry, 1 tablespoon brown sugar, white vinegar, water, soy sauce, and remaining onion powder. Simmer for 3 to 4 minutes, stirring often. Stir in the sesame oil, remove from heat, cover, and set aside.
6. During the last 45 minutes of cooking time, baste the chicken every 15 minutes with the sauce until the chicken reaches an internal temperature of 165°F.
7. Remove from the cooker and serve immediately.

SMOKEMASTER TIP: Sugar burns at 265°F, so keeping the grill temperature low and slow when using sweet rubs or sauces is vital to prevent burning.

COMPETITION CHICKEN THIGHS

PREP TIME: 30 minutes, plus 30 minutes to marinate / **Cook time:** 2 hours 10 minutes

At barbecue competitions, you can turn in any piece of chicken for judging. Almost everyone uses chicken thighs. They take on smoke perfectly and have the best bite when presented to the judges. Winning a barbecue competition requires practice and precision. This recipe might not get you the trophy right away, but it will help you on the path to the stage. Feel free to change up the sauce made in step 7 and use whatever barbecue sauce you like. The Blood Orange BBQ Sauce (page 173) goes great with chicken thighs.

SERVES 6

SUGGESTED WOOD: Oak, Cherry, Apple

½ cup coarse salt
⅓ cup white sugar
3 tablespoons freshly ground black pepper
1 tablespoon granulated garlic, plus ½ teaspoon
4 tablespoons sweet paprika, divided
2 teaspoons onion powder
1 teaspoon dry mustard
12 bone-in, skin-on chicken thighs
½ cup chicken broth
6 tablespoons butter, cut into 12 pieces

CONTINUED >

1. In a medium bowl, combine the salt, sugar, pepper, 1 tablespoon of granulated garlic, 1 tablespoon of paprika, onion powder, and dry mustard. Set aside.
2. Place each chicken thigh on a cutting board, bone-side down. Trim excess skin away. The skin should be like a blanket laying over the thigh but not wrapping over the ends or underneath. Remove any visible fat.
3. Apply the spice rub to the chicken thighs, then refrigerate for 30 minutes.
4. Preheat the grill or smoker to 250°F and prepare for indirect cooking. Depending on your cooker type, add your choice of wood chunks or smoke packet.
5. Remove the thighs from the refrigerator and discard any excess marinade. Place the thighs bone-side down onto the cooking grate. Cook for 1 hour.

2 cups ketchup
¾ cup brown sugar
⅓ cup water
¼ cup apple cider vinegar
3 tablespoons honey
2 tablespoons chili powder
1 teaspoon cayenne pepper
½ teaspoon salt

6. After 1 hour, transfer the chicken thighs to a large disposable aluminum pan. Pour the chicken broth into the pan. Place 1 piece of butter on top of each thigh and return to the grill or smoker. Continue cooking for another hour.

7. Meanwhile, in a medium saucepan over low heat, combine the ketchup, brown sugar, water, apple cider vinegar, remaining 3 tablespoons of paprika, honey, chili powder, cayenne, remaining ½ teaspoon of granulated garlic, and salt. Simmer for 10 minutes. Remove from heat and cover until ready to use.

8. When the thighs have reached an internal temperature of 165°F, remove them from the cooker and coat thickly with the barbecue sauce. Return the thighs to the cooker, placing them directly on the cooking grate. Cook for an additional 10 minutes. Remove and serve.

SMOKEMASTER TIP: The biggest challenge with cooking competition-quality chicken is getting the skin tender enough to bite through cleanly. Crispy is not desired here. One strategy is to peel the skin back before cooking and scrape with a sharp knife to remove all of the fat. This creates a thin skin that will cook quickly and evenly.

BOURBON BBQ CHICKEN LEGS

PREP TIME: 20 minutes / **Cook time:** 1½ hours

If you're new to smoking meats, try cooking up these sweet, tangy Bourbon BBQ Chicken Legs. They take little time to make, but the bourbon glaze is simply amazing. These are a crowd favorite.

SERVES 5

SUGGESTED WOOD:
Cherry, Apple

For the chicken

10 chicken legs
2 tablespoons olive oil
⅓ cup Poultry Rub (page 166)

For the sauce

2 tablespoons olive oil
½ sweet onion, chopped
2 garlic cloves, minced
1 cup tomato sauce
¾ cup packed brown sugar
½ cup water
¼ cup bourbon
¼ cup apple cider vinegar
2 teaspoons soy sauce
1 teaspoon Worcestershire sauce
2 teaspoons Poultry Rub
2 tablespoons butter

To make the chicken

1. Preheat the grill or smoker to 275°F. Depending on your cooker type, add your choice of wood before placing the chicken on to cook.
2. Trim away loose or excess skin from the chicken legs. Blot them dry with paper towels and brush with olive oil. Season the chicken legs liberally with the Poultry Rub.
3. Place the chicken into the cooker, close the lid, and cook for 1½ hours, or until they reach an internal temperature of between 175°F and 180°F.

To make the sauce

4. In a medium saucepan, heat the olive oil over medium-low heat. Add the onion and cook for 2 to 3 minutes, stirring often. Add the garlic and cook for 1 minute. Next, add the tomato sauce, brown sugar, water, bourbon, apple cider vinegar, soy sauce, Worcestershire sauce, and Poultry Rub.

5. Reduce the heat to low, cover, and let the sauce simmer for 10 to 12 minutes. Then transfer to a blender (or use an immersion blender) and puree the mixture. Return the sauce to the pan, and simmer uncovered over low heat for 10 to 15 more minutes, stirring occasionally. Once the sauce has reduced and thickened, remove the pan from heat, stir in the butter, cover, and keep warm.
6. After the chicken has cooked for 45 minutes, baste it with barbecue sauce every 10 to 15 minutes until done. Plate it up and serve.

SMOKEMASTER TIP: You can substitute the bourbon in this recipe for 2 tablespoons apple cider vinegar and 2 tablespoons peach nectar. Don't have peach nectar on hand? Any sweet fruit juice will do, but the milder the flavor, the better.

SMOKY CHICKEN WINGS

PREP TIME: 20 minutes / **Cook time:** 2 hours 5 minutes

Smoky chicken wings are incredibly flavorful. However, the skin runs the risk of turning out rubbery in the smoker. For this reason, this recipe uses two methods to crisp the skin. The first involves adding baking powder to the rub, and the second calls for broiling the wings for 4 to 5 minutes toward the end of the cooking time to crisp them up.

SERVES 8

SUGGESTED WOOD: Cherry, Apple, Hickory

4½ pounds chicken wings (flats and drumettes)
2 tablespoons salt
2 tablespoons dried oregano
1½ tablespoons cayenne pepper (adjust level to your liking)
1½ tablespoons freshly ground black pepper
1½ tablespoons onion powder
1 tablespoon granulated garlic
2 teaspoons baking powder

1. Preheat the grill or smoker to 250°F. Depending on your cooker type, add your preferred wood chips or chunks.
2. Lightly blot the wings with paper towels.
3. Combine the salt, oregano, cayenne, black pepper, onion powder, granulated garlic, and baking powder in a small bowl. Season the wings on all sides with the mixture.
4. Place the wings into the smoker, close the lid, and cook for 2 hours, or until the internal temperature reaches 165°F. Then remove the wings, and place on an aluminum cooking sheet or in a large disposable aluminum pan.
5. Increase the heat of your cooker to 450°F. Place the wings back into the smoker or grill, close the lid, and broil them for 5 minutes, or until skin begins to crisp up. Remove and serve with ranch or blue cheese dressing on the side.

SMOKEMASTER TIP: If your smoker is taking its sweet time heating up in step 5, broil the wings in your oven at 500°F for 5 minutes. Keep a close eye on them so that they do not burn. To change up the flavor of these chicken wings and make prep work easier, replace the dry rub with the Poultry Rub (page 166) and add the baking powder to the rub.

HOLIDAY TURKEY

PREP TIME: 20 minutes, plus 24 hours to brine / **Cook time:** 4 to 5 hours

One of the great secrets to the perfect holiday turkey is a brine. This means you need to start your turkey prep a day before you cook, but the rewards are great. The festive flavors matched with a good dose of smoke will make this a holiday favorite.

SERVES 8

SUGGESTED WOOD: Cherry, Apple

2 quarts apple juice
1 pound brown sugar
1 cup coarse kosher salt
3 quarts cold water
2 oranges, quartered
4 ounces fresh ginger, thinly sliced
15 whole cloves
4 bay leaves
4 garlic cloves, crushed
1 (12- to 14-pound) turkey
¼ cup olive oil

1. Combine the apple juice, brown sugar, and salt in a large stockpot. Bring to a boil over high heat and stir until the sugar and salt are completely dissolved. Remove from the heat and allow to cool for 30 minutes.
2. Add the water, oranges, ginger, cloves, bay leaves, and garlic.
3. Remove the giblets from the turkey and place the turkey in the brine mixture. Cover and refrigerate for 24 hours.
4. Preheat the grill or smoker to 300°F and set it for indirect cooking. Depending on your cooker type, add your choice of wood chunks or smoke packet to the fire.
5. Remove the turkey from the brine and rinse in cold water. Discard the brine.
6. Place the turkey on a roasting rack inside a roasting pan and place it on the grill or smoker.

CONTINUED >

7. Cook the turkey for 2 hours, then brush the surface of the turkey with the olive oil and continue cooking.
8. The turkey should take between 18 and 20 minutes per pound to cook. Adjust the cooking time accordingly. After 4 hours, begin checking the turkey for doneness. The turkey is cooked when all parts reach at least 165°F, but continue cooking until the thighs reach above 175°F for best results.
9. Remove the turkey from the cooker when done. Cover with foil and then a kitchen towel. Allow to rest for 20 to 30 minutes in a warm place. Carve and serve.

SMOKEMASTER TIP: Smoking very large turkeys can be a challenge. We generally smoke at temperatures lower than we bake. If you need a large amount of turkey for your meal, consider smoking two smaller turkeys instead of one very large one. The cooking times will be reduced and the flavor is generally better.

HERB-MARINATED TURKEY BREAST

PREP TIME: 30 minutes, plus 4 to 12 hours to marinate **/ Cook time:** 3½ hours

This is a great turkey recipe for when you are entertaining a small group. Look for a whole bone-in, skin-on breast. Instead of brining as in the recipe for Holiday Turkey (page 99), this recipe utilizes the power of marinating in two ways: on the surface via the rub and internally using an injection marinade. If you do not have a meat injector, skip this step. You can also wet brine the turkey in lieu of the injection marinade (see the SmokeMaster Tip). For a super simple version of this herb-marinated turkey, replace the dry rub ingredients below with the All-Purpose Rub (page 165).

SERVES 8

SUGGESTED WOOD:
Apple, Peach

½ cup low-sodium chicken broth, warmed
2 tablespoons unsalted butter, melted
1 tablespoon freshly squeezed lemon juice
½ teaspoon granulated garlic
½ teaspoon salt
¼ teaspoon white pepper
¼ cup unsalted butter, softened
2 teaspoons garlic salt

CONTINUED >

1. Combine the chicken broth, melted butter, lemon juice, granulated garlic, salt, and white pepper in a small bowl to make the injection marinade. Set aside.
2. In a separate small bowl, combine the softened butter, garlic salt, chili powder, rosemary, thyme, onion powder, paprika, celery salt, and black pepper.
3. Trim any loose skin from the turkey breast, keeping the main body of skin intact.
4. Draw some of the marinade into a food-safe meat injector. Insert it into the breast and slowly release the liquid. Repeat 3 to 4 more times at different angles.

CONTINUED >

- 2 teaspoons chili powder
- 1 teaspoon chopped fresh rosemary
- 1 teaspoon chopped fresh thyme
- 1 teaspoon onion powder
- 1 teaspoon paprika
- ½ teaspoon celery salt
- ½ teaspoon freshly ground black pepper
- 1 (5- to 6-pound) whole bone-in, skin-on turkey breast

5. Blot the turkey breast dry with paper towels, then apply the rub all over and under the skin. Place it into a large plastic baking bag, remove the air, and seal tightly. Refrigerate for 4 to 12 hours.
6. Preheat the grill or smoker to 250°F. Depending on your cooker type, add your choice of wood.
7. Remove the turkey breast from the refrigerator and discard the excess marinade. Place the breast into the cooker, close the lid, and cook for 3½ hours, or until the internal temperature at the thickest part of the meat reaches 165°F.
8. Once the turkey breast is cooked, remove from the cooker and cover with foil. Let the meat rest for 10 to 15 minutes, carve, and serve with cranberry sauce or gravy on top.

SMOKEMASTER TIP: If you prefer to brine the turkey instead of using the injection marinade, combine 9 cups cool water with ½ cup kosher salt and ½ cup white sugar. Stir until the salt and sugar have dissolved. Place the turkey breast in the brine, cover, and refrigerate for 12 to 18 hours. Remove, lightly rinse off the meat, season (omit salt from rub), and cook as directed.

BACON-WRAPPED TURKEY BREAST

PREP TIME: 30 minutes, plus 24 hours to brine / **Cook time**: 3 hours

Another fantastic turkey recipe for small gatherings, this Bacon-Wrapped Turkey Breast is everything you can ask for in a holiday meal. Brined, seasoned in a savory rub, wrapped in bacon, and cooked low and slow, this is a dish you'll want to make year after year.

SERVES 6

SUGGESTED WOOD: Cherry, Maple, Apple

3 quarts cold water
½ cup kosher salt
⅓ cup brown sugar
½ tablespoon whole peppercorns
2 garlic cloves, unpeeled and crushed
2 to 3 bay leaves
1 (3- to 3½-pound) boneless, skinless turkey breast
1 teaspoon paprika
1 teaspoon freshly ground black pepper
1 teaspoon onion powder
1 teaspoon dried sage
½ teaspoon granulated garlic
12 thin-cut bacon slices

1. In a large plastic tub or bowl, combine the water, salt, and brown sugar. Add the peppercorns, smashed garlic cloves, and bay leaves. Submerge the turkey breast in the brine, cover with a lid or plastic wrap, and refrigerate for 24 hours.
2. Preheat the grill or smoker to 250°F. Depending on your cooker type, add your choice of wood.
3. Remove the turkey breast from the brine, lightly rinse under cold water, and blot dry with paper towels.
4. In a small bowl, combine the paprika, black pepper, onion powder, dried sage, and granulated garlic. Season the breast all over with the rub.

CONTINUED >

5. Lay out the bacon on a cutting board, side by side in an even layer. Lay the turkey breast on top of the bacon, then fold the bacon over top of the turkey breast and secure with toothpicks. In narrower areas, use kitchen shears to cut the bacon to fit. Gently roll the wrapped breast over. The toothpicks will be on the bottom.
6. Place the turkey breast into your smoker or grill, close the lid, and cook for 3 hours, or until the internal temperature at the thickest part of the breast reaches 165°F. The bacon should be brown. If you have room, set a disposable aluminum pan underneath the breast to catch the bacon drippings.
7. Once cooked, remove the turkey and place on a clean cutting board. Tent with aluminum foil and let the meat rest for 15 minutes. Gently turn the breast on its side and remove the toothpicks. Carve and serve.

SMOKEMASTER TIP: Choose the flavor of bacon that suits your preferences for this dish. For a smokier finish, wrap with hickory-smoked bacon, or use maple- or applewood-smoked bacon for a bit of sweetness.

SWEET AND TANGY TURKEY LEGS

PREP TIME: 30 minutes, plus 12 to 18 hours to brine / **Cook time**: 3 to 4 hours

Most of us have tried and love those delicious festival and theme park turkey legs. Now you can make them right at home in your smoker. This recipe requires a long brine time, but it's well worth the wait. Remember to omit the salt from the Beef and Game Rub recipe before using on the turkey.

SERVES 4

SUGGESTED WOOD: Hickory, Maple, Cherry

8 cups water
½ cup bourbon
½ cup kosher salt
½ cup white sugar
2 bay leaves
4 cups ice, plus more if needed
4 turkey legs
¼ cup sriracha or other chili sauce
⅔ cup brown sugar
½ cup Beef and Game Rub (page 167), salt omitted
½ cup apple juice
¼ cup apple cider vinegar

1. In a large stockpot over medium-high heat, add the water, bourbon, salt, and white sugar. Simmer for 3 to 4 minutes. Remove from heat and add the bay leaves and ice. Let the mixture cool completely. Add another cup of ice if needed. Once cooled, submerge the turkey legs in the brine, cover, and place into the refrigerator for 12 to 18 hours.
2. Preheat the grill or smoker to 250°F. Depending on your cooker type, add your preferred wood.
3. Remove the legs from the brine and lightly rinse them under cold water. Blot dry with paper towels. Brush about 1 tablespoon of sriracha onto each leg.
4. In a medium bowl, combine the brown sugar with the saltless Beef and Game Rub. Apply the rub all over the turkey legs.
5. Place the turkey legs into the smoker or grill, close the lid, and cook for 3 to 4 hours, or until the internal temperature reaches 165°F.

CONTINUED >

6. Pour the apple juice and apple cider vinegar into a spray bottle. After 1½ to 2 hours of cook time, spritz the legs with this mixture every 30 minutes.
7. Once cooked, place the legs on a large platter or cutting board. Tent with foil, and let them rest for 10 minutes before digging in.

SMOKEMASTER TIP: Not all turkey legs are created equal. Similar to the size disparity between 12- and 20-pound turkeys, there will be size differences in the legs. Try to purchase comparable sizes so they cook at the same rate. If you opt for larger legs, be aware that they might take an hour or two longer to reach 165°F.

CARAMELIZED ORANGE DUCK

PREP TIME: 25 minutes, plus 12 to 15 hours to brine / **Cook time**: 2 to 2½ hours

This is a simple recipe for preparing smoked duck on your grill or smoker. It requires few ingredients, but the duck does need time to dry brine before cooking. The broiling process at the end takes place in your oven. So, plan ahead and preheat the oven for a seamless transition between smoker to oven.

SERVES 3 TO 4

SUGGESTED WOOD:
Cherry, Peach

1 (4- to 5-pound) duck
⅓ cup kosher salt
½ cup orange marmalade
2 tablespoons freshly squeezed lemon juice
¼ cup maple syrup
2 tablespoons water
1 teaspoon soy sauce
Pinch ground cloves

1. Remove the giblets from inside the duck. Blot the duck dry with paper towels and set on a baking sheet. Using a metal skewer or sturdy toothpick, puncture the skin (but not the flesh) several times all over the duck, and rub it with salt. Place the sheet with the duck into the refrigerator, uncovered, for 12 to 15 hours.
2. Preheat the grill or smoker to 275°F. Depending on your cooker type, add your preferred wood.
3. Once brined, remove the duck from the refrigerator and wipe away the salt with paper towels. Blot the surface dry.
4. Place the duck into your cooker, close the lid, and cook for 2 to 2½ hours, or until the internal temperature in multiple spots reads 160°F.

CONTINUED >

5. Meanwhile, in a small saucepan over medium heat, bring the orange marmalade, lemon juice, maple syrup, water, soy sauce, and cloves to a simmer. Stir until all the marmalade and maple syrup have melted and incorporated and the mixture is heated through. Cover and keep warm.
6. Preheat the oven to broil when the duck is almost done cooking. Baste the duck with the orange sauce and place it under the broiler for a few minutes until it caramelizes. Let the duck rest for 10 minutes, carve, and plate. If you have leftover orange sauce, serve it on the side.

SMOKEMASTER TIP: If your grill or smoker accommodates it, we recommend using a disposable pan to collect the drippings. Since duck has a thick layer of fat, it will render quite a bit during the cooking process.You can pour some of the duck fat over the duck once it's finished cooking, or use the duck fat in another recipe.

SOY-MARINATED DUCK BREASTS

PREP TIME: 15 minutes, plus 4 to 5 hours to marinate / **Cook time:** 2½ hours

This quick and easy recipe for delicious, marinated duck breasts both brines and smokes them to perfection. They are juicy, delicious, and great for any occasion.

SERVES 8

SUGGESTED WOOD:
Maple, Cherry

4 boneless, skin-on duck breasts
1 quart apple juice
2 tablespoons coarse kosher salt
2 tablespoons brown sugar
2 tablespoons soy sauce
1 teaspoon onion powder
1 teaspoon paprika
1 teaspoon granulated garlic
1 teaspoon dried marjoram
½ teaspoon five-spice powder
½ teaspoon white pepper

1. Place the duck breasts into a large plastic bowl or glass baking dish.
2. In a large bowl, combine the apple juice, salt, sugar, soy sauce, onion powder, paprika, granulated garlic, marjoram, five-spice powder, and white pepper, and stir until the salt and sugar have dissolved. Pour the marinade over the duck breasts, seal with plastic wrap, and refrigerate for 4 to 5 hours.
3. Preheat the grill or smoker to 250°F. Depending on your cooker type, add your wood of choice.
4. Remove the duck breasts from the refrigerator and discard the excess marinade. Lightly pat the duck breasts dry, then place them into the smoker skin-side up, close the lid, and cook for 2½ hours, or until the breasts reach an internal temperature of between 140°F and 150°F (medium to medium-well).
5. Remove from the smoker, place onto a cutting board, and tent loosely with aluminum foil. Rest them for 10 minutes, slice, and serve.

SMOKEMASTER TIP: The FDA recommends that all poultry be cooked to 165°F. However, some people enjoy medium-rare duck breast that is cooked to between 130°F and 135°F. You are more than welcome to pull it at this point.

EASY DUCK LEGS

PREP TIME: 20 minutes, plus 12 hours to brine / **Cook time**: 3 hours

These duck legs are simply seasoned, dry brined, and then hit with a bit of smoke. This recipe, using only salt and pepper to season, allows the succulent flavor of the duck to shine through. We recommend using equal-sized duck leg quarters to ensure even cooking.

SERVES 4

SUGGESTED WOOD:
Cherry, Apple

- 4 duck leg quarters, Muscovy or Pekin
- 2 tablespoons kosher salt, divided, plus more as needed
- 2 teaspoons freshly ground black pepper

1. Pat the duck legs dry with paper towels. Using a sharp skewer, prick the skin in several spots, making sure not to puncture the flesh. Rub each leg with ½ tablespoon kosher salt, then place them into a glass baking dish or large plastic container. Cover with plastic wrap, and refrigerate for 12 hours.
2. Preheat the grill or smoker to 250°F. Depending on your cooker type, add your desired wood.
3. Remove the duck legs from the refrigerator and wipe away the salt and moisture with paper towels. Season with black pepper.
4. Place the duck legs into your smoker, skin-side up, close the lid, and cook for 3 hours, or until they reach an internal temperature of 180°F. We recommend setting an aluminum pan under the grate to capture the rendered duck fat as the legs cook.
5. Once cooked, place the legs onto a plate or serving dish and let them rest for 15 minutes. Serve as is, or shred and use in other dishes.

SMOKEMASTER TIP: Not all rendered duck fat is suitable for cooking. You must make sure that it has reached a temperature of 190°F and that the flavor is palatable. If so, pour into a sterile glass jar, seal tight, and store in the refrigerator for up to a month.

APRICOT-GLAZED CORNISH GAME HENS

PREP TIME: 15 minutes / **Cook time:** 1½ to 2 hours

Cornish game hens are great for making a meal that looks fancy but is actually quick and easy. We use a simple apricot glaze to give these hens a sweet flavor with a pinch of heat. Add in a nice smoke flavor and these will quickly become a family favorite.

SERVES 4

SUGGESTED WOOD:
Hickory, Oak

- 4 Cornish game hens
- 2 tablespoons olive oil, divided
- 1 tablespoon salt, divided
- 1 tablespoon freshly ground black pepper, divided
- 1 cup apricot jam
- 1 tablespoon dry mustard
- 1 tablespoon sherry vinegar
- 2 tablespoons olive oil
- ¼ teaspoon cayenne pepper

1. Trim any loose pieces of skin from the hens. Brush each one with ½ tablespoon olive oil and season with salt and pepper. Set aside.
2. Preheat the grill or smoker to 225°F with indirect cooking.
3. Place the hens on the cooking grates. Depending on your cooker type, add any desired wood chunks or smoke packets and close the lid.
4. Meanwhile, prepare the glaze by combining the apricot jam, dry mustard, sherry vinegar, olive oil, and cayenne in a small saucepan over low heat. Warm through for about 10 minutes or until well combined.
5. Once the hens reach a temperature of 165°F (about 1½ to 2 hours), brush them liberally with the apricot glaze and continue cooking until the glaze forms a thick, sticky surface, about 10 minutes.
6. Remove, rest for 5 to 10 minutes, and serve.

SMOKEMASTER TIP: When smoking smaller items, it can be easier to place everything in a smoker-safe cooking dish. You can use disposable aluminum pans or cast-iron cookware. If you are using cast iron, handle with heat-resistant gloves.

QUAIL WITH PLUM GLAZE

PREP TIME: 15 minutes, plus 2 to 2½ hours to marinate / **Cook time:** 1 hour

Smoked quail is incredibly tender and delicious. They cook quickly and can be made in your smoker in as little as an hour. We recommend brining them in buttermilk first to keep them moist and tender throughout the cooking process. If you don't have plum jam on hand, use apricot jam instead. And to change up the flavor profile entirely, use the Pineapple Soy Glaze (page 174) instead of the plum glaze, half for basting and half for serving (you may have to double the recipe).

SERVES 8 TO 10

SUGGESTED WOOD:
Peach, Apple

For the glaze and sauce

2 cups red plum jam
¼ cup white vinegar
2 tablespoons brown sugar
1 to 2 teaspoons chili-garlic sauce
½ teaspoon onion powder
¼ teaspoon granulated garlic
2 tablespoons butter

For the quail

8 cups cool water
8 cups buttermilk
1 cup kosher salt
½ cup maple syrup
8 to 10 (4-ounce) semi-boneless quail
2½ tablespoons Beef and Game Rub (page 167)

To make the glaze and sauce

1. Combine the plum jam, white vinegar, brown sugar, chili-garlic sauce, onion powder, and granulated garlic in a small saucepan. Bring to a simmer over medium-high heat for 1 minute, stirring often. Reduce the heat to low and simmer for an additional 2 to 3 minutes. Remove from heat and stir in the butter. Divide the sauce, reserving half for basting and half to use for serving.

To make the quail

2. Combine the water, buttermilk, kosher salt, and maple syrup in a large kitchen-safe tub with a lid or a large bowl. Submerge the quail in the mixture. Cover and place in the refrigerator for 2 to 2½ hours.
3. Preheat the grill or smoker to 225°F. Depending on your cooker type, add your choice of wood.
4. Rinse the quail in cool water to remove the brine, and discard the excess brine. Pat the quail dry with paper towels and place them into a large disposable aluminum pan.

5. Season the quail with Beef and Game Rub. Next, wrap the legs with foil. Since quail legs are smaller than the rest of the body, they cook faster and run the risk of drying out.
6. Place the pan into the smoker or grill, close the lid, and cook for 30 minutes. After 30 minutes, remove the foil from the legs and baste the quail with half of the plum glaze. Close the lid and continue cooking for another 30 minutes, or until the quail reaches an internal temperature of 160°F.
7. Remove from the heat and let rest for 5 to 10 minutes. Serve with the remaining plum glaze on the side.

SMOKEMASTER TIP: You can also wrap the legs with bacon to add extra flavor and keep the legs from drying out. We recommend thin-cut bacon for the job.

CHAPTER 5

SEAFOOD

Plank Cooking

The grilling plank offers two good features for outdoor cooking.

First, it is a perfect way to grill or smoke delicate or small foods that might otherwise fall through the cooking grates. Fish fillets that might break apart easily on a cooking grate can smoke comfortably on a plank. Similarly, smaller items, like scallops, shrimp, or mussels, are also great for the plank.

Second, wood planks are heated during the cooking process, releasing smoke and wood flavor, the amount of which can be controlled by soaking the plank before cooking, which will reduce the amount of smoke produced and add a little extra moisture to the cooking environment. A dry plank over low heat will produce more smoke and even a little wood charring that can affect the flavor of more delicate meats.

If you want to cook fast or use the plank for extra smoke, we recommend putting it on the grill or smoker while the cooker preheats. Doing this will allow the plank to come to temperature. Place the food directly on the plank, close the lid, and cook. Once done, you can serve straight off the plank for a little extra presentation.

CEDAR PLANK FIRECRACKER SALMON

PREP TIME: 20 minutes, plus 1 hour to marinate **/ Cook time:** 1 hour

Salmon lends itself to low and slow cooking, and this easy cedar plank smoked salmon is great for those new to smoking fish. After the relatively quick cooking time, you will have a delicious, delicately smoked salmon that will impress even professional chefs.

SERVES 4

SUGGESTED WOOD: Cedar

4 (6-ounce) salmon fillets
2 tablespoons reduced-sodium soy sauce
2 tablespoons vegetable oil
2 tablespoons balsamic vinegar
1 tablespoon chili sauce
1 tablespoon brown sugar
½ teaspoon sesame oil
2 scallions, chopped, white and green parts separated
2 garlic cloves, minced
1 teaspoon grated fresh ginger
¼ teaspoon salt
1 large untreated cedar plank, or 2 small ones

1. Place the salmon fillets, skin-side down, into a glass baking dish. In a medium bowl, whisk together the soy sauce, vegetable oil, balsamic vinegar, chili sauce, brown sugar, sesame oil, the white parts of the scallions, garlic, ginger, and salt. Pour the sauce evenly over the salmon. Cover the dish with plastic wrap and refrigerate for 1 hour. At the same time, soak the cedar plank in tepid water for 1 hour.
2. Preheat the grill or smoker to 225°F. Depending on your cooker type, add a small amount of wood chunks or chips to the fire.
3. Once preheated, place the presoaked plank on the grate to heat up, about 4 to 5 minutes. Once it becomes aromatic, place the marinated salmon pieces on the plank, skin-side down, close the lid, and cook for 1 hour, or until the internal temperature of the salmon reaches 140°F. Remove from the smoker and serve immediately.

SMOKEMASTER TIP: When your plank-cooked items are done, lift the plank with everything on it off the grill and place it onto a sheet of aluminum foil. Fold the foil around the edges and use it as a serving platter.

SALMON CANDY

PREP TIME: 20 minutes, plus 27 hours to cure / **Cook time:** 3 to 4 hours

Cured in a mixture of brown sugar and kosher salt, then basted with maple syrup while smoking, Salmon Candy is truly a delicious treat. The process is not dissimilar to the low-temperature smoking of jerky. Salmon Candy is just as versatile and makes a great travel snack.

SERVES 8

SUGGESTED WOOD:
Maple, Alder

- 2¼ cups brown sugar
- 1½ cups kosher salt
- 5 pounds skin-on salmon, cut into 1½-inch strips
- 1¼ cups real maple syrup

SMOKEMASTER TIP: If you want more of a jerky-like texture and flavor, smoke the fish for 5 to 6 hours.

1. In a medium bowl, combine the brown sugar and salt. Fill a large glass dish or resealable plastic container ¼ inch deep with the mixture. Place the strips, skin-side down, into the mixture. Spread them out a little, as the salmon will need room to cure. If you need to build another layer, repeat the process with ¼ inch of the curing mixture between the layers. Cover and refrigerate for 2 hours.

2. Remove the fish, rinse it off under cold water, and blot dry with paper towels. Place the strips in a clean dish or pan and let them dry in the refrigerator for 24 hours uncovered.

3. Preheat the grill or smoker to 165°F. Depending on your cooker type, add your choice of wood.

4. Place the salmon strips directly onto the grates, and if your cooker has space, set an aluminum drip pan underneath the fish. Gradually bring the temperature up to 200°F over the span of 1 hour. Go no higher. Smoke the fish for 3 to 4 hours total, depending on thickness and desired texture. Every 90 minutes, brush the salmon with the maple syrup.

5. Once cooked, the candied salmon will have a deep color with a shiny finish. Remove from the smoker and place onto cooling racks for 1 hour before serving or eating. Store in the refrigerator or freezer in a vacuum-sealed bag.

ALDER-SMOKED SALMON STEAKS

PREP TIME: 20 minutes / **Cook time:** 1 hour

Salmon steaks differ from salmon fillets in a few ways. First, steaks are cut vertically through the bone section, while fillets are cut parallel to the bone. Second, because of their shape, steaks hold together better, tend to be juicier, and contain more fat toward the two pointed regions called the belly section.The garlic and Dijon mustard sauce is a simple yet delicious one that can be used in any number of recipes, including poultry and other seafood. For a different take, replace the ingredients in step 2 with the All-Purpose Rub (page 165). We like to make a double or triple batch of the All-Purpose Rub to have on hand; this cuts down on prep work and saves time.

SERVES 4

SUGGESTED WOOD: Alder

2 tablespoons olive oil
2 tablespoons Dijon mustard
2 teaspoons freshly ground black pepper
1 teaspoon sea salt
2 garlic cloves, minced
4 salmon steaks
1 untreated alder plank, soaked in water for 1 hour

1. Preheat the grill or smoker to 250°F. Depending on your cooker type, add a handful of alder wood to the fire.
2. In a small bowl, combine the olive oil, mustard, black pepper, salt, and garlic. Spoon about 1 tablespoon of the mixture onto each salmon steak. Gently work it onto both sides of the steak.
3. Remove the alder plank from the water, pat dry, and place the salmon steaks on top. Place the plank into your smoker or grill, close the lid, and cook for 1 hour, or until the internal temperature of the fish reaches 140°F.
4. Once cooked, remove from the heat and serve.

SMOKEMASTER TIP: You can smoke these salmon steaks without a plank. Start by oiling the grates of your grill or smoker and placing the fish right on the grates—cook as instructed and use a wide metal spatula to remove the fish.

CURED AND HOT-SMOKED SALMON

PREP TIME: 15 minutes, plus 10 to 17 hours to brine / **Cook time:** 1 to 1½ hours

The smoked salmon you buy at the grocery store is cured and cold smoked but typically not cooked. This is a traditional method for preserving fish but requires equipment that many people don't have. This hot smoked salmon is cooked but still has all the flavor you would expect. The secret is in the formation of a pellicle on the surface of the salmon. This is vital to a great smoked fish, but don't worry, we'll walk you through the process.

SERVES 6

SUGGESTED WOOD:
Oak, Hickory

- 4 cups ice-cold water
- ¼ cup kosher salt
- ¼ cup brown sugar
- 2 bay leaves
- ½ cup chopped fennel
- 2 tablespoons dried onion
- 2 teaspoons granulated garlic
- 2 pounds salmon fillets

1. In a large bowl, combine the water, salt, brown sugar, bay leaves, fennel, dried onion, and granulated garlic. Stir until the salt and sugar are completely dissolved.
2. Place the salmon fillets in a glass baking dish, skin-side down. Pour the brine mixture over top. Cover and refrigerate for 6 to 12 hours.
3. Remove the fillets from the brine, rinse them in cold water, and pat dry with paper towels.
4. Place the fillets on a clean plate or dish. Place them in a cool, well ventilated space or your refrigerator for 4 to 5 hours, uncovered. This will cause the surface of the fish to turn opaque, creating what is known as the pellicle. This layer absorbs smoke better.

5. Preheat the grill or smoker to a temperature between 180°F and 200°F with indirect cooking.
6. Place the salmon fillets on the cooker. Depending on your cooker type, add additional wood chunks or smoke packets. Smoke for 1 to 1½ hours, or until the salmon reaches an internal temperature of 140°F. Remove and serve.

SMOKEMASTER TIP: These smoked salmon fillets can be used the same way as cold-smoked salmon. Keep them refrigerated in an airtight container and use within 5 days of smoking, or seal in an airtight bag and freeze for up to 6 months.

SOY-MARINATED TUNA STEAKS

PREP TIME: 20 minutes, plus 1 hour to marinate / **Cook time:** 1 to 1½ hours

Soy sauce is a great base for a marinade because it's packed with flavor, and since it already has substantial salt content, you don't need to use any additional salt. The tuna steaks absorb the flavors of the garlic, ginger, and citrusy orange juice beautifully. This marinade would go well with a number of other proteins as well, including chicken, steak, or halibut.

SERVES 4

SUGGESTED WOOD:
Cherry, Apple

4 (7- to 8-ounce) ahi tuna steaks
½ cup reduced-sodium soy sauce
Juice of 1 navel orange
1 tablespoon mirin or dry sherry
2 tablespoons brown sugar
3 garlic cloves, minced
2 teaspoons grated fresh ginger
1 teaspoon onion powder
1 teaspoon sesame oil
½ teaspoon white pepper

1. Place the tuna steaks into a resealable plastic bag. In a medium bowl, whisk together the soy sauce, orange juice, mirin or sherry, brown sugar, garlic, ginger, onion powder, sesame oil, and white pepper. Pour the mixture over the tuna steaks, making sure they are well coated. Seal the bag and refrigerate for 1 hour.
2. Preheat the grill or smoker to 225°F. Depending on your cooker type, add your choice of wood.
3. Remove the tuna steaks from the marinade, place directly onto the grates, close the lid, and cook for 1 to 1½ hours, or until the internal temperature reaches 140°F.
4. Remove the steaks from your cooker and let stand for a few minutes before serving.

SMOKEMASTER TIP: Most of us are familiar with grilled tuna steaks that are rare on the inside with a nice, seared crust on the outside. These smoked tuna steaks, however, are completely different. Slow smoked, the tuna is tender and delicious, full of flavor. Use these steaks in a Niçoise salad or as a substitute for smoked salmon in your favorite recipes.

SMOKED WHOLE TROUT

PREP TIME: 15 minutes, plus 6 to 12 hours to brine **/ Cook time:** 1½ to 2 hours

The secret to a great smoked trout is a good brine. The brine enhances the flavor and adds the perfect amount of savory sweetness. You will need to plan ahead for this recipe, but it is very easy to make and doesn't take up a lot of room on the grill or in the smoker.

SERVES 4

SUGGESTED WOOD: Alder

2 quarts water
½ cup kosher salt
½ cup brown sugar
2 whole, medium-sized trout
2 tablespoons butter
8 lemon slices

SMOKEMASTER TIP: Smoked trout is the perfect ingredient in many dishes. Take the meat of one trout fillet and combine it with 4 ounces cream cheese, ¼ cup sour cream, and fresh chives. This makes a fantastic dip for any occasion.

1. In a large bowl, combine the water, salt, and sugar and stir until completely dissolved.
2. Place the trout in a shallow dish and pour the brine over top. Cover and refrigerate for 6 to 12 hours.
3. Preheat the smoker or grill to a temperature between 200°F and 225°F.
4. Remove the trout from the brine and rinse with cold water. Place 1 tablespoon of butter and 4 lemon slices inside each fish.
5. Place the trout on the grill or smoker. Depending on your cooker type, add any additional wood chunks or smoke packets.
6. Smoke for 1½ to 2 hours, or until the internal temperature of the fish reaches 160°F.
7. Remove from the grill or smoker, gently open the fish, and remove the lemon slices. The bones will separate from the fish as it cooks and should be easy to remove. The skin will easily peel away from the fillets. Serve immediately.

GARLIC BUTTER SEA BASS

PREP TIME: 20 minutes / **Cook time:** 1 to 1½ hours

Sea bass, especially the Chilean variety, has a tender texture and buttery flavor. It's even better slow smoked. Keep an eye on the internal temperature of the fish to avoid overcooking. If you can, purchase the sea bass fresh. Some frozen fish and seafood do not thaw well and produce less than stellar results. Our advice is to find a good fishmonger in your area.

SERVES 4

SUGGESTED WOOD: Apple, Alder, Cherry

- ½ teaspoon sea salt
- ¼ teaspoon onion powder
- ¼ teaspoon paprika
- ¼ teaspoon freshly ground black pepper
- 2 pounds fresh sea bass fillets, Chilean or Atlantic
- 3 tablespoons butter
- Juice of 1 large lemon
- 1 tablespoon finely chopped flat-leaf parsley, plus more for serving
- 2 garlic cloves
- 1½ tablespoons extra-virgin olive oil

1. Preheat the grill or smoker to 200°F. Depending on your cooker type, add your preferred wood a few minutes before cook time.
2. Combine the sea salt, onion powder, paprika, and pepper in a small bowl. Sprinkle onto the exposed flesh of the fish. Then, place the fish directly onto the smoker or grill grates, close the lid, and cook for 1 to 1½ hours, or until the internal temperature at the thickest part of the fish reaches 140°F.
3. Meanwhile, in a small saucepan over medium heat, combine the butter, lemon juice, parsley, and garlic and cook for 2 minutes.
4. During the second half of the cook time, begin brushing the fish with the butter sauce every 15 minutes until it has cooked through.
5. Remove the fish, plate it up, drizzle the olive oil on top, and garnish with chopped parsley before serving.

SMOKEMASTER TIP: Want it a little smokier? If your cooking equipment allows it, try smoking this sea bass at 170°F to 180°F until done.

HERB-STUFFED SNAPPER

PREP TIME: 20 minutes, plus 4 hours to marinate **/ Cook time:** 1 hour

Red snapper has been a favorite recipe to cook around the campfire. With this recipe, we take it to the smoker to amp up the flavor.

SERVES 4

SUGGESTED WOOD:
Mesquite

For the marinade

Juice and zest of 1 lime
¼ cup olive oil
¼ cup white wine
2 teaspoons chopped fresh thyme
2 teaspoons chopped fresh oregano
1 teaspoon salt
1 teaspoon freshly ground black pepper
½ teaspoon red pepper flakes

For the snapper

1 (4- to 6-pound) whole red snapper
2 limes, sliced
Pinch salt
Pinch freshly ground black pepper
1 small red onion, sliced
1 small orange, sliced

To make the marinade

1. In a medium bowl, combine the lime juice and zest, olive oil, wine, thyme, oregano, salt, pepper, and red pepper flakes. Set aside until ready to use.

To make the snapper

2. Place the snapper on a cutting board. Make diagonal slits every inch down the side of the fish starting behind the gills. Stuff lime slices into the slits. Turn the fish over and repeat. Season the snapper inside and out with salt and pepper.
3. Stuff the inside of the fish with the red onion and orange slices. Place the snapper in a shallow dish and pour the marinade over top.
4. Cover and refrigerate the snapper for 4 hours. Turn over halfway through the marinating time.
5. Preheat the grill or smoker to 250°F with indirect cooking. Add your choice of wood chips or smoke packet to the fire.
6. Place the snapper on the indirect portion of the grill or smoker and cook for 1 hour, or until it reaches an internal temperature of 160°F.

SMOKEMASTER TIP: As with any fish, handling this red snapper can be challenging. We recommend using an oversized spatula or a pair of spatulas. Lift the fish gently and slide a platter or cutting board under it.

SMOKED COD FILLETS

PREP TIME: 20 minutes, plus 2 hours to marinate / **Cook time:** 45 minutes to 1 hour

These smoked cod fillets are easy to prepare, quick to cook, and can be enjoyed on their own or in a variety of recipes. Try serving them over rice or use as a delicious filling for fish tacos.

SERVES 6

SUGGESTED WOOD:
Alder, Apple

6 (6-ounce) cod fillets
¼ cup olive oil
Juice of 2 limes
2 garlic cloves, minced
2 teaspoons honey
2 teaspoons ancho chile powder
2 teaspoons ground cumin
1 teaspoon onion powder
1 teaspoon sea salt
½ teaspoon freshly ground black pepper

1. Place the cod fillets into a glass baking dish, flesh-side up. In a medium bowl, combine the olive oil, lime juice, garlic, honey, chile powder, cumin, onion powder, salt, and black pepper. Pour the mixture over the fish, then cover with plastic wrap and refrigerate for 1 hour.
2. Remove the fillets from the marinade and gently blot away excess marinade. Place them onto a large plate or platter and put them back into the refrigerator uncovered for another hour.
3. Preheat the grill or smoker to 225°F. Depending on your cooker type, add your choice of wood.
4. Place the fillets directly onto the grates, close the lid, and cook for 45 minutes to 1 hour, or until the internal temperature of the cod reaches 145°F.
5. Using a metal spatula, gently work the fillets away from the grates and place them onto a clean cutting board or serving dish. Serve immediately.

SMOKEMASTER TIP: Foods that have a short cook time will have a light smoke flavor. You can amp up the smoke flavor by adding more wood chunks to a charcoal fire, smoke packets to a gas grill, or smoke tubes for pellet grills. Smoke tubes are easy to find and act as an independent smoke source for all types of outdoor cooking.

CATFISH WITH COMEBACK SAUCE

PREP TIME: 10 minutes, plus 4 hours to marinate / **Cook time:** 1 hour

We marinate these catfish fillets to enhance the flavors and keep them tender as they smoke. The real treat of this recipe, however, is our Comeback Sauce that is served with the smoked catfish. There's a reason it's called "comeback" sauce. You'll definitely want to come back for more!

SERVES 4

SUGGESTED WOOD:
Hickory, Pecan

For the catfish

½ cup olive oil
3 tablespoons honey
3 tablespoons white vinegar
2 tablespoons chopped fresh dill
1 tablespoon mild chili powder
2 teaspoons dried rosemary, crushed
4 (6- to 7-ounce) catfish fillets

To make the catfish

1. In a medium bowl, combine the olive oil, honey, vinegar, dill, chili powder, and rosemary.
2. Rinse the catfish fillets and pat dry with paper towels. Place the catfish in a shallow dish or a resealable bag and pour the marinade over top. Flip to coat evenly. Cover the dish and refrigerate for 4 hours.
3. Preheat the grill or smoker to 250°F with indirect cooking. Depending on your cooker type, add your choice of wood chunks or smoke packet to the fire.
4. Remove the fillets from the marinade, and blot away any excess with paper towels. Place the fillets directly on the cooking grate and smoke for 1 hour. Add any additional wood chunks or smoke packets along with the fish.

CONTINUED >

For the sauce

1 cup mayonnaise
¼ cup chili sauce
¼ cup ketchup
2 tablespoons olive oil
Juice of 1 medium lemon
1 teaspoon Creole or spicy mustard
1 teaspoon Worcestershire sauce
1 garlic clove, minced
½ teaspoon Cajun seasoning
¼ teaspoon onion powder
Pinch salt
Pinch freshly ground black pepper
2 to 3 dashes hot sauce

To make the sauce

5. Combine the mayonnaise, chili sauce, ketchup, olive oil, lemon juice, mustard, Worcestershire sauce, garlic, Cajun seasoning, onion powder, salt, pepper, and hot sauce in a small bowl. Stir to mix well and refrigerate until ready to use.

6. When the catfish fillets reach 145°F, remove them from the grill or smoker and serve immediately with Comeback Sauce on the side.

SMOKEMASTER TIP: Fish fillets can be a challenge to cook on an open cooking grate. We recommend putting fillets on a wire cooling rack for extra support. Place the fillets on the rack and then transport the rack to the grill. When the fish is cooked, use heat-resistant gloves to lift the rack off the grill and place it on a large cutting board.

CHILI-LIME SHRIMP

PREP TIME: 30 minutes / **Cook time:** 30 minutes

These jumbo shrimp are coated with a flavorful barbecue rub, smoked fast, and tossed with a simple lime-butter sauce. This is a great appetizer item that also pairs well with the Rib Eye Steak with Rosemary-Garlic Butter (page 26).

SERVES 4

SUGGESTED WOOD:
Hickory, Pecan

1 pound jumbo shrimp, peeled and deveined
1 tablespoon chili powder
2 teaspoons salt
2 teaspoons onion powder
2 teaspoons granulated garlic
2 teaspoons freshly ground black pepper
1 teaspoon dried oregano
½ cup butter
1 tablespoon freshly squeezed lime juice
2 scallions, green parts only, chopped

1. Preheat the grill or smoker to 250°F. Depending on your cooker type, add your wood of choice to the fire.
2. Combine the chili powder, salt, onion powder, granulated garlic, black pepper, and oregano in a small bowl. Season the shrimp on both sides with the rub.
3. Lay the shrimp on an aluminum baking sheet or disposable pan, place it into your grill or smoker, close the lid, and cook for 30 minutes, or until the shrimp turn pink and have an internal temperature of 120°F.
4. Using your stovetop or side burner, melt the butter in a small saucepan over medium heat. Add the lime juice and stir through.
5. Once the shrimp have cooked, pour the lime-butter mixture into the pan, toss with tongs to coat, garnish with scallions, and serve immediately.

SMOKEMASTER TIP: Look for fresh shrimp whenever possible. Shrimp that smells fishy or like ammonia are most likely not fresh and should not be used. If buying frozen shrimp, look for ones with the shell still on. Shrimp that has been peeled and deveined prior to freezing are more likely to be mushy when thawed.

LOBSTER TAILS WITH DRAWN BUTTER

PREP TIME: 10 minutes / **Cook time:** 40 minutes

Lobster is usually cooked hot and fast. Of course, steamed can also mean bland, so here we take our lobster tails to the grill or smoker and add a hit of smoke. Add fresh herbs, tangy citrus, and drawn butter, and you have the best lobster tails you've ever eaten.

SERVES 4

SUGGESTED WOOD: Hickory, Oak

1 cup butter
2 tablespoons olive oil
1 tablespoon freshly squeezed lemon juice
3 to 4 garlic cloves, minced
2 teaspoons finely chopped fresh basil
⅛ teaspoon salt
⅛ teaspoon freshly ground black pepper
4 (8- to 10-ounce) lobster tails

1. Melt the butter in a large saucepan over medium-high heat until foam starts to collect on the surface, 4 to 5 minutes. Reduce the heat to low and cook for an additional 8 to 10 minutes, or until the milk solids settle at the bottom of the pan. Pour the butter through a cheesecloth-lined strainer or sieve into a bowl. Cover and set aside.
2. Preheat the grill or smoker to 250°F.
3. Combine the olive oil, lemon juice, garlic, basil, salt, and pepper in a small bowl. Set aside.
4. Using kitchen shears, cut the lobster shells on the very top of the tail from the cut end to where the tail fans out. Fold open the shell carefully (it's sharp) to expose the flesh underneath. Lift the meat portion out and set it on top of the shell. Do not remove it completely; you just want to shift its position upward.
5. Brush ¼ of the olive oil-herb mixture onto the exposed meat portion of each lobster tail.

6. Place the tails on the cooking grate. Depending on your cooker type, add your choice of wood chunks or smoke packets. Close the lid and cook for 40 minutes, or until the internal temperature reaches between 135°F and 140°F.
7. Once the lobster tails are cooked, remove them from your cooker, and serve with the drawn butter.

SMOKEMASTER TIP: Start your dinner off right by looking for the right kind of lobster. Cold-water lobster is readily available in the United States in all shapes and sizes. Remember that good lobster flesh is shiny and milky white in appearance. Avoid any product that is enhanced or has green or brown discoloration on the flesh.

SMOKY CRAB CLUSTERS

PREP TIME: 10 minutes / **Cook time:** 25 minutes

Amazingly enough, smoke penetrates the shell of these crab clusters, so you can get all that extra flavor easily on the grill or smoker. If you are using frozen crab clusters, let them thaw overnight in the refrigerator before cooking.

SERVES 4

SUGGESTED WOOD: Oak, Fruitwood

1 cup melted butter
1 teaspoon salt
1 teaspoon freshly ground black pepper
½ tablespoon ground coriander
2 teaspoons dried oregano
1 teaspoon garlic powder
2 to 3 pounds snow crab clusters

1. Preheat the grill or smoker to 225°F and set your cooker for indirect grilling.
2. Combine the butter, salt, pepper, coriander, oregano, and garlic powder in a large saucepan over low heat. Stir until melted through, then remove from heat and cover to keep warm.
3. Dip the ends of the crab clusters into the butter sauce and then place directly on the grill or smoker. Smoke for 20 to 25 minutes, basting the clusters with the butter sauce every 10 minutes. The shells should be bright in color and the meat should be opaque white.
4. Remove from the cooker and serve hot, or place on ice and serve cold.

SMOKEMASTER TIP: Put your saucepan with the butter mixture right in the grill or smoker. With this recipe, keeping the butter mixture warm prevents the butter from solidifying. But when you apply the butter to the crab as it's cooking, you want to find a cooler corner of the grill or smoker to place the pot so the butter doesn't boil. Use a cast-iron or heavy metal saucepan that is oven-safe. And remember—it will be hot!

SMOKED OYSTERS

PREP TIME: 15 minutes, plus 20 minutes to soak **/ Cook time:** 1 hour

Smoked oysters have a bad reputation because of the canned version. However, these smoked oysters are fresh and packed with flavor. They make a fantastic appetizer or a main dish, and they're incredibly versatile—use them in any of your favorite recipes.

SERVES 6

SUGGESTED WOOD: Alder, Cherry, Apple

40 fresh oysters in the shell
1 cup dry white wine
1 cup water
¼ cup good-quality olive oil

1. Rinse the oysters in cold water. In a large pot, bring the wine and water to a boil. Add the oysters in small batches to the boiling liquid. Remove the oysters as they open. Any oyster that doesn't open in 3 minutes should be discarded.
2. Once all the oysters are open, strain the boiling liquid through a paper towel, coffee filter, or cheesecloth, and reserve.
3. With a knife, cut each oyster from the shell and drop it into the liquid. Allow them to soak for 20 minutes.
4. Preheat the grill or smoker to the lowest temperature you can maintain, around 175°F or lower if possible. Depending on your cooker type, add your choice of wood chips or smoke packet to the fire. Place the oysters on a fine baking rack that won't let the smaller oysters fall through. Transfer to the smoker or grill and smoke for 1 hour. Remove the oysters from the smoker or grill, toss with the olive oil, and enjoy.

SMOKEMASTER TIP: These smoked oysters are superior to any canned variety. You can store these oysters in the refrigerator in a sealed glass jar for up to 1 week or freeze them for up to 6 months.

PLANKED SCALLOPS

PREP TIME: 20 minutes, plus 1 hour to soak / **Cook time:** 30 minutes

If you're a fan of scallops, you will love this recipe. And if you're not—this recipe just might make you a fan! These plank-smoked scallops are tossed in a delicious lemon-garlic butter sauce right before serving. This dish makes a fantastic appetizer or main course for special occasions.

SERVES 2 TO 3

SUGGESTED WOOD:
Alder, Oak

1 large untreated alder or oak plank, soaked in water for 1 hour
8 to 10 large sea scallops
1½ tablespoons olive oil
¼ teaspoon salt
½ teaspoon freshly ground black pepper
¼ cup butter
2 garlic cloves, minced
Juice of 1 large lemon
¼ teaspoon onion powder
Pinch salt
Pinch red pepper flakes
2 tablespoons chopped flat-leaf parsley

1. Preheat the grill or smoker to 200°F. Depending on your cooker type, add your choice of wood.
2. Remove the plank from the water and blot excess moisture with paper towels.
3. Rinse the scallops under cold water, and trim off the small white muscle tags. Blot dry.
4. In a medium bowl, combine the olive oil, salt, and black pepper. Add the scallops and toss gently to coat.
5. Arrange the scallops on the plank and place into the grill or smoker, close the lid, and cook for 20 to 30 minutes (depending on the cooker used), or until the scallops reach an internal temperature of 125°F.
6. Meanwhile, in a skillet over medium heat, melt the butter, then add the garlic and cook for 30 seconds. Next, add the lemon juice, onion powder, salt, and red pepper flakes. Cook for 2 minutes, until the sauce begins to reduce.

7. Add the smoked scallops right into the pan with the sauce, and gently turn to coat. Garnish with the chopped parsley and serve immediately.

SMOKEMASTER TIP: Keep a close eye on the scallops as they cook. This process can go quickly, and the scallops can turn from tender to chewy in a matter of minutes. The ideal doneness temperature is 125°F, but you can pull the scallops at 120°F and add them straight to the sauce. The carryover heat will bring them to 125°F in no time.

CHAPTER 6

SMOKED SIDES AND DESSERTS

Smoke 'Em If You've Got 'Em

When it comes to smoking, we tend to think about the big proteins, like briskets and pork roasts. But there are so many other foods that can benefit from a kiss of smoke. Best of all, many basic side dishes and desserts are relatively easy to smoke. Want a simple smoky dessert? Try taking a tube of cookie dough from the grocery store, make extra-big cookies, and put them in the smoker for 25 minutes at 300° F. Top with ice cream for a quick and easy dessert.

For simple but delicious side dishes, any vegetable that you would cook in the oven can be cooked in a smoker. Keep the temperature low and adjust the cooking times as needed. Keep a few extra disposable aluminum pans on hand, and you can make smoky, buttery carrots in 30 minutes. Try your favorite recipe for potatoes or vegan alternatives like tofu on the smoker. Remember that a smoker is a low-temperature oven. It roasts and bakes with the added flavor of smoke. Take advantage of the extra space in your smoker and add some side dishes as you cook your main meal.

We recommend using cast-iron skillets, disposable aluminum pans, or other smoker-safe cookware. Smoke can discolor light-colored cookware, making it hard to clean.

MAC 'N' CHEESE

PREP TIME: 15 minutes / **Cook time:** 1½ hours

There is nothing quite like the creamy goodness of macaroni and cheese, but if you're interested in taking it up a notch, put it on the smoker for next-level flavor.

SERVES 5 TO 6

SUGGESTED WOOD: Apple, Pecan, Cherry

1 stick (8 tablespoons) butter, plus ¼ cup melted butter, divided
¼ cup all-purpose flour
2 teaspoons Dijon mustard
2¼ cups half-and-half
4 ounces cream cheese
2½ cups shredded cheddar cheese
1 cup shredded Gouda cheese (not smoked)
½ cup shredded Parmesan cheese
1 tablespoon plus ¼ teaspoon salt, divided
¼ teaspoon freshly ground black pepper
¼ teaspoon garlic powder
¼ teaspoon onion powder
12 ounces dry macaroni
1 cup panko bread crumbs
3 bacon slices, cooked and crumbled

1. Preheat the grill or smoker to 225°F. Prepare for a 1-hour cook time.
2. In a medium saucepan over medium heat, melt the stick of butter. Stir in the flour and cook until the mixture thickens and forms a roux, 1 to 2 minutes. Add the Dijon, then whisk in the half-and-half. Add the cream cheese, cheddar, Gouda, Parmesan, ¼ teaspoon of salt, pepper, garlic powder, and onion powder.
3. Meanwhile, bring a large pot of water to a boil with the remaining 1 tablespoon of salt and cook the noodles according to package directions.
4. Drain the macaroni, add to the cheese mixture, then place into a 19-by-9-inch aluminum pan.
5. In a medium bowl, combine the panko, ¼ cup melted butter, and crumbled bacon. Top the macaroni and cheese with the panko-bacon mixture.
6. Place the pan into the smoker, close the lid, and cook for 1 hour.
7. Once done, remove the pan and serve immediately.

SMOKEMASTER TIP: Keep the temperature low throughout the cooking process, so the noodles don't dry out. The cheese sauce for this recipe is thick. If you'd like a thinner sauce, consider using ¼ to ½ cup more half-and-half.

COWBOY BEANS

PREP TIME: 20 minutes / **Cook time:** 2 hours 15 minutes

These smoky and sweet baked beans make a hearty meal that can be served as the main course or side dish. This easy-to-make recipe starts on the stovetop and is then transferred to the smoker for the rest of the cook time.

SERVES 6

SUGGESTED WOOD: Apple, Cherry, Maple

- 6 slices raw bacon, diced
- 1 medium yellow onion, diced
- 1 serrano pepper, seeded and diced
- 3 garlic cloves, minced
- ½ pound ground beef
- 1 (20-ounce) can baked beans
- 1 (15-ounce) can white beans (great northern or white chili beans)
- 1¾ cups barbecue sauce
- ⅓ cup plain cola
- 3 tablespoons brown sugar
- 3 tablespoons ketchup
- 1 tablespoon Worcestershire sauce
- ½ teaspoon freshly ground black pepper
- ½ teaspoon cayenne pepper (optional)

1. Prepare the grill or smoker for a 250°F-degree, 2-hour cook time. Add your choice of wood chunks or smoke packet to the fire.
2. Place a large cast-iron skillet on the stovetop over medium heat. Cook the diced bacon until browned and the fat has rendered. Remove the bacon from the pan and set it aside, leaving the bacon fat in the skillet.
3. Add the onion and serrano to the skillet and sauté for 2 minutes. Add the garlic and the ground beef and cook for an additional 5 minutes, or until the ground beef is no longer pink.
4. Turn off the heat and stir in the baked beans, white beans, barbecue sauce, cola, brown sugar, ketchup, Worcestershire sauce, black pepper, and cayenne (if using).
5. Transfer the skillet to the smoker, uncovered. Close the lid and cook for 2 hours at 225°F to 250°F.
6. After 2 hours, use heat-resistant gloves to remove the skillet from the smoker and serve.

SMOKEMASTER TIP: Have leftover brisket or smoked pork? Chop it up and use it in this recipe instead of ground beef.

GARLIC BUTTER CAULIFLOWER

PREP TIME: 15 minutes / **Cook time:** 50 minutes

This is a recipe that appeals to both vegetarians and meat eaters alike. A simple recipe that's not short on flavor, the cauliflower is smoked whole and seasoned with a simple mix of salt, garlic powder, and lemon pepper. It's a great starting point to smoking vegetables, and with just a few ingredients, you can prepare it in a snap.

SERVES 4 TO 6

SUGGESTED WOOD:
Maple, Hickory

1 (3- to 4-pound) head of cauliflower
2 tablespoons olive oil
1½ teaspoons sea salt
1 teaspoon garlic powder
1 teaspoon lemon pepper
3 tablespoons melted butter

1. Preheat the grill or smoker to 275°F. Depending on your cooker type, add your choice of wood chunks or smoke packet to the fire.
2. Wash the cauliflower and trim off the leaves. Brush liberally with the olive oil. In a small bowl, combine the salt, garlic powder, and lemon pepper, and season the cauliflower all over. Set it into a large skillet or aluminum pan.
3. Place into the smoker, close the lid, and cook for 45 to 50 minutes. The cauliflower is done when it is tender but still firm.
4. Remove the cauliflower from the smoker and either break into florets or cut into slices. Drizzle with the melted butter and serve.

SMOKEMASTER TIP: Smoked cauliflower isn't just a great side dish. When sliced, it can be used as a meat substitute for your vegetarian guests. Use a slice to replace a burger patty or any other meat at your cookout. Omit the melted butter at the end and top with barbecue sauce for a smokier flavor. If you have a batch of All-Purpose Rub (page 165) on hand, use that to season the cauliflower in place of the salt, garlic powder, and lemon pepper in this recipe.

SOUTHERN-STYLE POTATO SALAD

PREP TIME: 20 minutes, plus 1 hour to cool / **Cook time:** 1 hour

This go-to summer side dish is made even better once it meets the smoker. We bypass boiling the potatoes and smoke them instead. Southern-style potato salad never tasted so good.

SERVES 6

SUGGESTED WOOD: Hickory, Mesquite

- 2 pounds russet potatoes
- Olive oil, for brushing
- 1⅔ cups mayonnaise
- 2 scallions, chopped
- 2 tablespoons relish
- 1½ tablespoons Dijon mustard
- 1½ tablespoons white vinegar
- 1½ teaspoons salt
- ½ teaspoon onion powder
- ¼ teaspoon white sugar
- ¼ teaspoon garlic powder
- ¼ teaspoon freshly ground black pepper
- ¼ teaspoon smoked paprika
- 3 hard-boiled eggs, chopped

1. Preheat the grill or smoker to 200°F, with good smoke production. Depending on your cooker type, add your choice of wood chunks or smoke packet to the fire.
2. Wash and dry the potatoes, then brush them with olive oil. Using a skewer or small knife, puncture each potato 5 to 7 times to the center. Place into the smoker for 30 minutes.
3. After 30 minutes, remove the potatoes and finish cooking in a 450°F oven. (If you are working with a pellet smoker, remove the potatoes and crank the heat up to 450°F. Place the potatoes back in and roast them for an additional 20 to 30 minutes, or until they are easily pierced with a knife.)
4. Once cooked, remove and let cool for 1 hour. Remove the skins and chop into 1-inch pieces. If you have time, you can also place the potatoes into the refrigerator for an hour after cooking. This will make the skinning and chopping process easier.

5. In a large bowl, combine the mayonnaise, scallions, relish, Dijon mustard, white vinegar, salt, onion powder, sugar, garlic powder, pepper, and smoked paprika. Taste and adjust salt as needed.
6. Add the potatoes and eggs, and gently fold to combine. Transfer to a serving dish, cover tightly, and refrigerate for 2 hours before serving.

VARIATION: This recipe uses a traditional creamy dressing, but any variation of potato salad can benefit from the smoky potatoes. Try this technique with your family favorite recipe. A simple dressing of olive oil, balsamic vinegar, and your favorite herbs, combined while the potatoes are still warm, makes a great hot potato salad.

HONEY-CINNAMON SWEET POTATOES

PREP TIME: 15 minutes / **Cook time:** 1½ to 2 hours

This is the perfect side dish for when you want just the right amount of sweetness. These Honey-Cinnamon Sweet Potatoes are simple to make and mouthwateringly delicious, especially when served with the honey-cinnamon butter.

SERVES 6

SUGGESTED WOOD: Maple

6 sweet potatoes
½ tablespoon olive oil
1 tablespoon kosher salt
½ stick (4 tablespoons) salted butter, at room temperature
2 tablespoons honey
1 teaspoon cinnamon

1. Prepare the grill or smoker for a 250°F, 2-hour cook time. Depending on your cooker type, add your choice of wood chunks or smoke packet to the fire.
2. Wash and dry the sweet potatoes. Pierce each potato 5 to 6 times using a skewer or fork. Brush with the olive oil and rub with the salt.
3. Place the potatoes directly onto the grates, close the lid, and cook for 1½ to 2 hours, or until tender. Remove and let stand for 10 minutes.
4. In a small bowl, mix the butter, honey, and cinnamon until well combined.
5. Make a lengthwise slit in each sweet potato, open them slightly, and top with 1 to 1½ tablespoons of the honey-cinnamon butter, then serve.

SMOKEMASTER TIP: While this recipe makes a great side dish as is, you can use it as the starting point to customize your favorite sweet potato dish. Keep this recipe handy to serve with your Holiday Turkey (page 99).

SMOKED WHOLE TOMATOES

PREP TIME: 15 minutes / **Cook time:** 45 minutes

This is a basic smoked tomato recipe that can be served as a side or in other recipes. Use them when making marinara sauce, salsa, pizza sauce, or turn them into a smoky tomato soup. See the variation tip following the recipe for more ideas.

SERVES 4 TO 5 AS A SIDE DISH

SUGGESTED WOOD: Apple, Pecan, Maple

16 plum tomatoes, halved lengthwise
Olive oil, for brushing
1 to 2 tablespoons salt

1. Prepare the smoker or grill for 225°F for indirect cooking. Add any additional wood chunks or smoke packets.
2. Brush tomato halves with olive oil and set them into a large aluminum pan. Season with the salt.
3. Place the pan into the smoker, close the lid, and cook for 45 minutes, or until tender.
4. Remove, and let the tomatoes cool before handling. Use as needed.

VARIATION TIP: To turn these tomatoes into your favorite sauce or soup, allow them to cool after cooking until comfortable to handle. The skins will be loose and easy to remove. Place into a blender and puree. Now you have a smoky tomato sauce that is ready for use in any recipe.

TEXAS TWINKIES (BACON-WRAPPED JALAPEÑOS)

PREP TIME: 30 minutes / **Cook time:** 2 hours

This recipe is a bestselling menu item at Hutchins BBQ in McKinney, Texas. These Texas Twinkies, or bacon-wrapped jalapeños, are a great way to use up those barbecue brisket leftovers. Jalapeños are stuffed with a meat and cheese filling, wrapped in bacon, glazed with sauce, and smoked to perfection—what could be better?

MAKES 12

SUGGESTED WOOD: Hickory, Mesquite, Pecan

- 12 large jalapeños
- 1 pound Beginner's Brisket (page 20), chopped
- 12 ounces cream cheese, softened
- ½ cup shredded white cheddar cheese
- 2 tablespoons chopped red onion
- ¼ teaspoon ground cumin
- ¼ teaspoon garlic powder
- Pinch salt
- Pinch freshly ground black pepper
- 12 thick-cut bacon slices
- 1½ cups barbecue sauce of choice
- Toothpicks

1. Wash and dry each jalapeño. Cut about ⅛ inch under the stem, piercing the jalapeño halfway. Then make a perpendicular cut lengthwise, forming a T shape, exposing the seeds and white flesh. Do not cut all the way through. Carefully scoop out the seeds and white flesh. Repeat with the remaining jalapeños, then set aside.
2. Prepare your grill or smoker for a 250°F, 2-hour cook time. Place the brisket in a food processor and pulse 5 to 6 times. It should resemble cooked ground beef. Remove the brisket and place in a large bowl along with the cream cheese, cheddar, onion, cumin, garlic powder, salt, and pepper and stir until thoroughly combined.
3. Fill each pepper with as much filling as it can take. Wrap each pepper with a slice of bacon and carefully secure with toothpicks. Place onto a large aluminum tray.

4. Place the tray of jalapeños on the grill grate. Close the lid and cook for about 1½ hours. During the last half hour, brush the barbecue sauce on the jalapeños, close the lid, and cook for 30 minutes.
5. Remove from heat and serve immediately.

SMOKEMASTER TIP: Use gloves when handling spicy peppers like jalapeños. Try using a piping bag to help fill these Texas Twinkies. Load up the bag and use a large piping tip to dispense the filling into the jalapeños. If you are a particular fan of this recipe, you can purchase a jalapeño rack for your smoker that will make cooking them much easier.

CREAMY ONION DIP

PREP TIME: 15 minutes, plus 1 hour to cool / **Cook time:** 1 hour

This is a perfect appetizer to make alongside the main dish. If you've already got the smoker running, why not just pop a few onions on there and make this creamy, cheesy onion dip? The onions need some time to cook and cool, but you'll have the dip assembled in no time.

SERVES 6 TO 8

SUGGESTED WOOD:
Hickory, Oak

2 medium yellow onions, halved vertically
Olive oil, for drizzling
8 ounces cream cheese, softened
¾ cup sour cream
¼ cup mayonnaise
1 tablespoon apple cider vinegar
2 tablespoons chopped fresh chives
1 tablespoon chopped fresh parsley
¼ teaspoon salt, plus more as needed
¼ teaspoon freshly ground black pepper
¼ teaspoon garlic powder

1. Preheat the grill or smoker to 250°F. Depending on your cooker type, add your choice of wood chunks or smoke packet to the fire.
2. Place the onion halves cut-side up into a large aluminum pan. Drizzle with the olive oil and place the pan on the smoker. Close the lid and cook for 1 hour, or until the onions are tender and have browned slightly.
3. Once cooked, remove from the smoker and let them cool for 1 hour. Chop into small pieces and set aside.
4. In a medium bowl, mix together the cream cheese, sour cream, mayonnaise, and apple cider vinegar. Fold in the chopped cooked onions, chives, parsley, salt, black pepper, and garlic powder. Mix to incorporate, then serve.

SMOKEMASTER TIP: For best results, refrigerate dip for at least 2 hours before serving.

MEATLOAF-STUFFED ONION BOMBS

PREP TIME: 25 minutes / **Cook time:** 1 hour

These onion bombs are essentially meatloaf meatballs sandwiched between onion layers, wrapped in bacon, then smoked. Full of flavor, they make quite a hearty meal all on their own.

SERVES 6 TO 7

SUGGESTED WOOD:
Hickory, Cherry

2 medium yellow onions
1 pound ground beef
½ cup bread crumbs
½ cup shredded cheddar cheese
½ cup shredded Parmesan cheese
1 large egg
1 tablespoon dried parsley
1 tablespoon ketchup
2 garlic cloves, minced
1 teaspoon Worcestershire sauce
1 teaspoon salt
½ teaspoon dried oregano
½ teaspoon freshly ground black pepper
12 thick-cut bacon slices
12 to 18 toothpicks
1 cup barbecue sauce of choice

1. Preheat the grill or smoker to 275°F. Add your choice of wood chunks or smoke packet to the fire.
2. Cut the ends off both onions, then slice down the center of the onions lengthwise. Remove the skins and soft outer layers. Separate the larger rings and match them with each other. Set aside.
3. In a large bowl, combine the ground beef with the bread crumbs, cheddar, Parmesan, egg, parsley, ketchup, garlic, Worcestershire sauce, salt, oregano, and pepper. Taking about ⅓ cup of the meat mixture, form it into a ball, then press it gently into one of the onion rings. Take the matching onion ring and place on top. Wrap the bomb with 1 to 2 strips of bacon and secure with toothpicks. Repeat the process until all the bombs are assembled.
4. Place onion bombs directly onto the cooking grate. Close lid and cook for 45 minutes. After 45 minutes, brush with barbecue sauce, then cook for another 20 to 30 minutes, or until they reach an internal temperature of 165°F.
5. Remove the bombs from the smoker and serve.

VARIATION TIP: Replace the Parmesan with pepper jack cheese and add some diced green chiles or jalapeños for a spicy version.

CHEESY HASH BROWN POTATOES

PREP TIME: 15 minutes / **Cook time:** 1 hour 15 minutes

Cheese and hash browns are a winning combination no matter what, but when you put this casserole on the smoker, it takes it to another level. This cheesy hash brown casserole is usually gone within minutes after serving—it's not a bad idea to double the recipe and make an extra pan.

SERVES 6 TO 7

SUGGESTED WOOD:
Alder, Apple

- 2 tablespoons olive oil
- 1 small yellow onion, diced
- 2 garlic cloves, minced
- 3 cups corn flake cereal, crushed
- ½ cup melted butter, divided
- 1 (30-ounce) bag frozen hash browns
- 1 (15-ounce) can cream of mushroom soup
- 1 cup shredded sharp cheddar cheese
- 1 cup sour cream
- ⅓ cup shredded Parmesan cheese
- ¼ cup mayonnaise
- 1 teaspoon salt
- ½ teaspoon freshly ground black pepper
- 1 (4-ounce) can diced mild green chiles (optional)

1. Prepare the grill or smoker for a 225°F, 1-hour-and 15-minute cook time.
2. On the stovetop, heat the oil in a large saucepan over medium heat. Add the onion and cook for 3 minutes, stirring often. Add the garlic and cook for 1 minute. Remove from the heat.
3. Prepare the topping by combining the crushed corn flake cereal with ¼ cup of melted butter in a large bowl.
4. In a separate bowl, combine the frozen hash browns with the remaining ¼ cup of melted butter, along with the cream of mushroom soup, sharp cheddar, sour cream, Parmesan, mayonnaise, salt, pepper, and chiles (if using). Fold to combine. Place the hash brown mixture into a large aluminum pan and top with the corn flake mixture.

5. Place the pan into the smoker, close lid, and cook for about 1 hour and 15 minutes, or until the sides of the casserole start to brown and pull away from the edges and the potatoes are tender.
6. Once cooked, remove casserole from the smoker and serve immediately.

SMOKEMASTER TIP: Leave the frozen hash browns on the counter for 30 minutes to defrost before starting the recipe. This will reduce clumping and make the hash browns easier to work with.

SMOKED CORN ON THE COB

PREP TIME: 20 minutes, plus 2 hours to soak / **Cook time:** 45 minutes to 1 hour

If you've never made smoked corn on the cob, what are you waiting for? Smoked corn is quite flavorful and is a great alternative to boiled, especially if you're already using the smoker to make another dish. Serve this as a side dish at your next potluck or barbecue—you'll have people coming back for more.

SERVES 6

SUGGESTED WOOD:
Hickory, Pecan

- 6 ears corn, husks intact
- 1 stick (8 tablespoons) unsalted butter, melted
- 2 teaspoons brown sugar
- 1½ teaspoons onion powder
- 1 teaspoon paprika (not smoked)
- 1 teaspoon chili powder
- 1 teaspoon salt
- ½ teaspoon garlic powder
- ½ teaspoon freshly ground black pepper

1. Carefully pull back the husks to expose the corn, but don't remove them. Remove the silk threads only. Place the corn in a large bowl with enough cool water to cover them. Let them soak for 2 hours.
2. Preheat the grill or smoker to 225°F. Depending on your cooker type, add your choice of wood chunks or smoke packet to the fire.
3. Remove the corn from the water and blot the husks and exposed kernels dry with a paper towel.
4. In a medium bowl, combine melted butter, brown sugar, onion powder, paprika, chili powder, salt, garlic powder, and pepper, and brush onto the corn kernels. Pull the husks back over the corn cobs.
5. Place the corn on the grill, close the lid, and cook for 45 minutes to 1 hour, or until the corn takes on a light golden-brown color and the husks have darkened.
6. Once done, remove the husks and serve the corn immediately.

SMOKEMASTER TIP: Garnish with chopped green onions and cotija cheese, or roll the smoked corn in butter and sprinkle with chopped herbs. This corn can be used in other recipes, for instance, corn salsa.

BACON BALSAMIC BRUSSELS SPROUTS

PREP TIME: 15 minutes / **Cook time:** 55 minutes

This recipe will make anyone a fan of Brussels sprouts. Combined with bacon, onions, and balsamic vinegar, this smoky, tangy side dish is bursting with flavor, and the bonus is the whole thing is prepared and cooked in about an hour.

SERVES 4 TO 5

SUGGESTED WOOD:
Cherry, Maple

6 thick-cut bacon slices
1 small yellow onion, thinly sliced
2 garlic cloves, finely chopped
1½ pounds Brussels sprouts, washed, stems and excess leaves removed
1 tablespoon olive oil
½ teaspoon salt
½ teaspoon freshly ground black pepper
2 tablespoons balsamic vinegar

1. Preheat the grill or smoker to 250°F. Depending on your cooker type, add your choice of wood chunks or smoke packet to the fire.
2. On the stovetop, cook the bacon in a large skillet over medium heat until the fat renders, about 7 minutes. Once cooked, remove the bacon and use 3 to 4 tablespoons of the bacon fat to sauté the onion. After 2 minutes, add the garlic and stir. Cook for another minute, then remove from heat.
3. Place the Brussels sprouts in a large aluminum pan with the onion and garlic.
4. Chop the bacon into small pieces and add to the Brussels sprouts. Add the olive oil, salt, and pepper to the pan and toss to combine.
5. Place the pan on the grill, close the lid, and cook for 45 minutes. Remove and drizzle with balsamic vinegar, then serve.

SMOKEMASTER TIP: If you have meat in the rack above, consider placing the Brussels sprouts below. Those drippings will help flavor them even more.

HOLIDAY STUFFING

PREP TIME: 15 minutes / **Cook time:** 1 hour 20 minutes

This smoked stuffing is a great addition to any holiday meal or Sunday dinner. We recommend using golden delicious apples to add a nice touch of sweetness to the savory elements of the stuffing.

SERVES 4 TO 5

SUGGESTED WOOD:
Pecan, Apple

2 tablespoons olive oil
12 ounces chicken-apple sausage, casings removed
1 small yellow onion, chopped
2 large celery stalks, chopped
2 garlic cloves, minced
16 ounces stuffing cubes, homemade or prepackaged
2 medium sweet apples, peeled, cored, and chopped
2 large eggs
3 cups vegetable broth
½ teaspoon dried sage
½ teaspoon salt
½ teaspoon dried rosemary
½ teaspoon red pepper flakes (optional)
3 tablespoons melted butter

1. Preheat the grill or smoker to 225°F. Depending on your cooker type, add your choice of wood chunks or smoke packet to the fire.
2. Heat the olive oil in a large skillet over medium heat on your stovetop. Add the sausage and sauté for 3 to 4 minutes. Add the onion, celery, and garlic and cook for 2 to 3 minutes, until the vegetables start to become tender. Stir in the stuffing cubes and apples. Remove from heat and set aside.
3. In a large bowl, whisk together the eggs, vegetable broth, sage, salt, rosemary, and red pepper flakes (if using). Add the contents of the skillet to the egg mixture and gently fold to combine. Place the stuffing in a large aluminum pan and drizzle with the melted butter.
4. Place the pan on the grill, close the lid, and cook for about 1 hour 20 minutes, or until the stuffing is browned and slightly crispy on top.
5. Remove and serve.

VARIATION TIP: If you'd like to substitute the apples, use ¾ cup dried cherries or cranberries instead.

SMOKED CORN PUDDING

PREP TIME: 20 minutes / **Cook time:** 50 minutes to 1 hour 5 minutes

Corn pudding is a savory Southern dish normally served from midsummer to winter. It's especially delicious when corn is in season and you can buy it fresh; however, canned or frozen corn will work in a pinch.

SERVES 6

SUGGESTED WOOD:

Cherry, Pecan

- 2 eggs
- 1 (12-ounce) can evaporated milk
- 2½ tablespoons all-purpose flour
- 2 tablespoons melted butter
- 1½ cups corn kernels (about 4 medium ears)
- 1 (15-ounce) can creamed corn
- 1 cup shredded cheddar cheese
- ½ cup shredded pepper jack cheese
- 2 teaspoons white sugar
- 1 teaspoon salt
- ½ teaspoon freshly ground black pepper
- 1 tablespoon vegetable oil

1. Preheat the grill or smoker to 300°F. Depending on your cooker type, add your choice of wood chunks or smoke packet to the fire.
2. In a large bowl, whisk together the eggs, evaporated milk, flour, and melted butter until well combined. Add the corn kernels, creamed corn, cheddar, pepper jack, sugar, salt, and black pepper. Stir to combine.
3. Grease a 19-by-9-inch aluminum pan with the vegetable oil and pour the corn mixture into it.
4. Place the pan on the grill, close the lid, and cook for 50 minutes. After 50 minutes, check to see if the center has set. If it is still soft, cook for an additional 10 to 15 minutes. The sides should be golden brown and the center slightly firm. Remove from the smoker and let stand for 10 minutes before serving.

VARIATION: You can use smoked or roasted corn for an additional kick of campfire goodness. If you want a spicier version, add chopped green chiles to the mixture in step 2. One or two jalapeños will give it a little extra heat without overpowering the dish.

CHANTILLY POTATOES

PREP TIME: 20 minutes / **Cook time:** 1 hour

Chantilly Potatoes are essentially next-level mashed potatoes—smoked, with cheese and cream. They are absolutely delicious and a gorgeous side dish for special occasions. The bonus is that they go with pretty much any main dish you're making!

SERVES 4 TO 5

SUGGESTED WOOD: Maple, Hickory

- 4 medium russet potatoes, peeled and cut into 1-inch cubes
- 1 cup heavy cream
- ½ cup butter, melted
- 1 cup shredded Gouda cheese
- 1 teaspoon salt
- ½ teaspoon freshly ground black pepper
- ¼ teaspoon garlic powder
- ½ cup shredded Parmesan cheese

1. Bring a large pot of water to a boil over high heat. Add the potatoes and boil until tender, about 20 minutes. Drain and mash the potatoes with a masher or fork.
2. Preheat the grill or smoker to 275°F. Depending on your cooker type, add your choice of wood chunks or smoke packet to the fire.
3. Place the cooked potatoes in a large bowl. Add the cream, melted butter, Gouda, salt, black pepper, and garlic powder. Taste and adjust salt as needed.
4. Scoop the mixture into a 19-by-9-inch aluminum pan and top with the Parmesan cheese.
5. Place the pan, uncovered, on the grill, close the lid, and cook for 40 minutes. The cheese will have melted and the potatoes will appear golden brown around the edges when done.
6. Remove and serve immediately.

SMOKEMASTER TIP: For even more flavor and presentation, after removing the pan from the smoker, place the whole dish under your oven broiler on high for 2 to 3 minutes. This will give the surface a little crunch and add texture to the potatoes.

SMOKED BUTTERNUT SQUASH

PREP TIME: 15 minutes / **Cook time:** 1 hour

This smoked butternut squash can be served as is, dressed up with some chopped fresh herbs, or topped with nuts. It's also perfect for adding extra flavor to soups, lasagnas, and sauces.

SERVES 4 TO 5

SUGGESTED WOOD: Alder, Cherry, Maple

2 butternut squash
3 tablespoons olive oil
1½ teaspoons coarse salt

1. Preheat the grill or smoker to 275°F.
2. Cut off the top inch or so of each squash, then slice them in half lengthwise. Leave the seeds intact. Brush the flesh with olive oil, and season with salt.
3. Place the butternut squash on the grill cut-side up, close the lid, and cook for 1 hour. The squash should be tender when done.
4. Remove and let it cool for at least 15 to 20 minutes before handling. Discard the seeds, scoop out the flesh, and use or store as needed.

SMOKEMASTER TIP: If you'd like your butternut squash a little less smoky, put it on the smoker for 30 minutes, and finish it off for 25 to 30 minutes in the oven at 350°F.

S'MORES DIP

PREP TIME: 15 minutes / **Cook time:** 15 minutes

Want that campfire s'mores flavor without the actual campfire? Use your smoker instead. The best part about this dish is that it's a shareable dip. Serve with graham crackers or cookies on the side.

SERVES 4 TO 5

SUGGESTED WOOD: Cherry, Maple, Pecan

12 ounces cookie butter
1 jar marshmallow fluff
1 cup chopped milk chocolate
⅓ cup crushed graham crackers
⅓ cup chopped pecans (optional)
Graham crackers or cookies, for dipping

1. Preheat the grill or smoker to 300°F. Depending on your cooker type, add your choice of wood chunks or smoke packet to the fire.
2. In a 12-inch cast-iron pan, layer the cookie butter, then the marshmallow fluff, chopped chocolate, crushed graham crackers, and nuts (if using).
3. Place on the grill, close the lid, and cook for 10 to 15 minutes. Keep an eye on it to make sure it doesn't burn. Once everything is melted through, remove and serve with graham crackers or cookies of your choice.

SMOKEMASTER TIP: Because of the short smoking time of this dish, you can assemble it in the pan and refrigerate until it is nearly time for dessert. Once it's melted through, take this straight from the smoker to the table so everyone can enjoy the chocolatey goodness.

CHOCOLATE SAUCE WITH A KICK

PREP TIME: 15 minutes / **Cook time:** 20 minutes

This smoked chocolate sauce will up your dessert game. A true multipurpose sauce, you can drizzle it over ice cream, grilled fruits, or crepes—the options are endless. The smoke flavor isn't overpowering but will add another layer of depth to the chocolate.

MAKES ABOUT 2 CUPS

SUGGESTED WOOD: Alder, Apple

- 1½ cups heavy cream
- ¾ cup semisweet chocolate chips
- ⅛ teaspoon cinnamon
- Pinch cayenne pepper (optional)

1. Preheat the grill or smoker to 250°F, with good smoke production. Depending on your cooker type, add your choice of wood chunks or smoke packet to the fire.
2. Pour the cream and chocolate chips into a medium cast-iron skillet. Place on the grill, close the lid, and cook for 10 minutes. Open the lid and give it a good stir. Place it back into the smoker and cook for an additional 5 to 10 minutes. Once the chocolate has melted and has incorporated with the cream, remove and stir in the cinnamon and cayenne (if using).
3. Remove from heat and serve immediately.

SMOKEMASTER TIP: Watch for burning. Let the sauce tell you when it is done.

APPLE CRISP

PREP TIME: 25 minutes / **Cook time:** 1 hour

If you've already got the smoker on, why not finish up the meal with a nice apple crisp? That little kiss of smoke really adds a nice punch to the classic combination of apples, brown sugar, and oats in this comforting dessert.

SERVES 5 TO 6

SUGGESTED WOOD: Apple, Maple, Pecan

- 5 Granny Smith apples, peeled, cored, and thinly sliced
- 1 tablespoon freshly squeezed lemon juice
- ¼ cup brown sugar, plus ⅓ cup
- 2 tablespoons white sugar
- 3 tablespoons melted butter
- 2 teaspoons vanilla extract
- ¾ teaspoon ground cinnamon, divided
- 1¼ cups old-fashioned oats
- ¼ cup flour
- 5 tablespoons cold butter, chopped
- ¼ teaspoon ground nutmeg
- Vegetable oil, for greasing

1. Preheat the grill or smoker to 350°F. Depending on your cooker type, add your choice of wood chunks or smoke packet to the fire.
2. In a large bowl, combine the apples, lemon juice, ¼ cup of brown sugar, white sugar, melted butter, vanilla, and ¼ teaspoon of cinnamon. Set aside.
3. In a food processor, combine the oats, flour, remaining ⅓ cup of brown sugar, cold butter, remaining ½ teaspoon of cinnamon, and nutmeg. Pulse 5 or 6 times.
4. Grease the inside of a medium cast-iron skillet with oil. Arrange the sliced apples in the bottom of the skillet, then top with the crumble mixture. Place the pan into the grill, close the lid, and cook for 1 hour.
5. Remove the pan and let cool for 15 minutes. Serve with a scoop of vanilla ice cream and a drizzle of warm caramel sauce.

VARIATION TIP: Want it sweeter? Use Gala, Fuji, or Honey Crisp apples instead.

CANDIED PINEAPPLE

PREP TIME: 15 minutes / **Cook time:** 1 hour

This smoked pineapple is infused with rum, rubbed with a brown sugar–cinnamon mixture, then smoked to perfection. You will need a food-safe injector for this recipe, which is available online and in kitchen supply stores. If you do not have an injector, you can marinate the whole pineapple for 20 minutes before cooking.

SERVES 4 TO 6

SUGGESTED WOOD:
Oak, Cherry

1 pineapple
½ cup dark rum
1 cup light brown sugar
1½ teaspoons ground cinnamon
½ teaspoon ground nutmeg

SMOKEMASTER TIP: Chop this smoked pineapple into smaller pieces and add to your favorite summertime cocktails.

1. Preheat the grill or smoker to 350°F. Depending on your cooker type, add your choice of wood chunks or smoke packet to the fire.
2. Cut the stem and skin off the pineapple, making it as close to a rectangular shape as possible.
3. Put the rum into a small bowl or cup. Draw some of it into the injector and slowly inject it into the pineapple in different sections, starting with the core and working around it.
4. In a small bowl, combine the brown sugar, cinnamon, and nutmeg.
5. Place the pineapple in a large aluminum pan and coat the top with half of the sugar mixture. Set in the smoker or grill and cook for 30 minutes.
6. Using heat-resistant gloves, carefully turn the pineapple over and sprinkle the remaining half of the sugar mixture on the opposite side. Close the lid and continue to cook for 30 more minutes. The pineapple will have a nice brown color and caramelization on its surface when done.
7. Remove and let it rest for 5 minutes. Transfer to a cutting board and slice into 1-inch-thick rounds. Serve with ice cream on top.

★ ★ ★ CHAPTER 7 ★ ★ ★

RUBS, BRINES, MARINADES, AND SAUCES

It's All in the Timing

Flavor begins before cooking. Whether using a simple seasoning or a long brine, the best way to improve smoked food is to add flavor before lighting the smoker.

In barbecue, we typically start with a rub. This is a combination of salt, spices, and sometimes sugar. Apply the rub early and let it sit for a more intense flavor or right before cooking to keep it subtle.

Wet and dry brines use salt, which alters the composition of meat, making it more tender. Add any flavor to a brine, and that will carry into the meat. Large cuts and whole poultry may require brining times up to 24 hours, while small cuts usually brine for a few hours.

Marinades are recommended for high-temperature cooking but still play a role in low and slow smoking. A classic example of a marinade resembles a vinaigrette that contains oil, vinegar, and seasonings. The type of meat, the density, and the size determine marinating times.

Glazes and sauces go on last and are optional—but encouraged! A good example would be barbecue ribs. When the rack is nearly cooked, it's time to sauce. This allows the sauce to cook onto the meat but not block the absorption of smoke.

ALL-PURPOSE RUB

PREP TIME: 10 minutes

This rub contains the perfect blend of flavors to complement all types of barbecued meats. It's a classic for a reason and balances perfectly with any smoked food. This is the one rub to keep on hand for all occasions.

MAKES 2¼ CUPS

½ cup brown sugar
⅓ cup paprika (not smoked)
¼ cup kosher salt
3 tablespoons mild chili powder
2 tablespoons ground cumin
2 tablespoons onion powder
2 tablespoons garlic powder
2 tablespoons dry mustard
1 tablespoon freshly ground black pepper
1 tablespoon cayenne pepper
2 teaspoons dried marjoram

Combine all ingredients in a medium-sized bowl and use as needed. Store in an airtight jar in the cupboard for up to 1 year.

USE WITH: All types of smoked meats but particularly pork shoulder or butt, beef or pork ribs, and poultry.

POULTRY RUB

PREP TIME: 10 minutes

Use this poultry rub on all types of poultry, from chicken to game birds. The flavor combination is mellow and will complement most smoked meats. This rub is great for use in marinades, bastes, and sauces.

MAKES ½ CUP

- 1 tablespoon paprika (not smoked)
- 1 tablespoon mild chili powder
- 1 tablespoon onion powder
- 1 tablespoon dry mustard
- 1 tablespoon dried parsley
- 1 tablespoon kosher salt
- 1 tablespoon celery salt
- 2 teaspoons herbes de Provence
- 2 teaspoons white sugar
- 1 teaspoon granulated garlic
- ½ teaspoon dried sage
- ¼ teaspoon allspice

Combine ingredients in a small bowl and use as needed. Make a double or triple batch and store in an airtight container in your pantry for up to a year.

USE WITH: Poultry, including whole chicken and turkey, chicken pieces, turkey legs, game hens, goose, and pheasant.

BEEF AND GAME RUB

PREP TIME: 15 minutes

This is a spicy rub with an earthy foundation that works perfectly with beef and game. You will need a spice grinder or a good mortar and pestle for this recipe.

MAKES ½ CUP

- 2 tablespoons whole peppercorns
- 1 tablespoon cumin seeds
- 1 tablespoon coriander seeds
- 2 tablespoons coarse, kosher, or sea salt
- 1 teaspoon granulated garlic
- ½ teaspoon smoked paprika
- ½ teaspoon cayenne pepper

1. In a small skillet over medium heat, toast the peppercorns, cumin seeds, and coriander seeds for 1 minute, or until fragrant. Shake the pan gently during the toasting process to avoid burning the spices.
2. Pour the toasted spices onto a plate and let them cool completely. Grind them in a spice grinder or use a mortar and pestle to pulverize them.
3. In a small bowl, mix the ground spices with the salt, granulated garlic, smoked paprika, and cayenne pepper. Use immediately or store in a closed container in the cupboard for up to a year.

USE WITH: Beef roasts, wild boar, venison roasts, steaks, and other game meats.

ALL-PURPOSE MARINADE

PREP TIME: 10 minutes

This recipe has all the components of a classic marinade, including readily accessible items you probably already have in your pantry. All you'll need is oil, vinegar, herbs, and spices. This marinade is easy to prepare and versatile. It can even double as a salad dressing or side sauce.

MAKES 1 CUP

⅔ cup red wine vinegar
2 garlic cloves, minced (or 1 teaspoon granulated garlic)
1 tablespoon salt
2 teaspoons freshly ground black pepper
2 teaspoons onion powder
1 teaspoon chopped fresh thyme (or ½ teaspoon dried thyme)
½ cup olive oil

Combine the vinegar, garlic, salt, pepper, onion powder, and thyme in a medium bowl. Slowly whisk in the olive oil to slightly thicken the marinade. Use immediately or store in an airtight container in the refrigerator for up to 1 week.

USE WITH: Large cuts of meat like beef chuck, pork shoulder, leg of lamb, or venison roasts. You can also use on a whole turkey, chicken and other poultry, steaks, chops, fish, and vegetables.

MARINATING TIMES

BEEF, PORK, AND VENISON ROASTS	12 to 24 hours
WHOLE POULTRY	8 to 16 hours
STEAKS AND CHOPS	4 to 8 hours
POULTRY PIECES	2 to 6 hours
FISH AND SEAFOOD	30 to 40 minutes
CHOPPED VEGETABLES	30 minutes

BRISKET INJECTION MARINADE

PREP TIME: 10 minutes

This is an injectable marinade used in thick cuts of meat, like brisket. Injecting the marinade into the meat's core adds flavor while balancing out moisture during the cooking process. You'll need a food-safe marinade injector for the job. They can be found online or in most grocery stores.

MAKES 1 CUP

1 cup beef broth
2 teaspoons Worcestershire sauce
2 teaspoons soy sauce
2 teaspoons brown sugar
½ teaspoon onion powder
½ teaspoon garlic powder
½ teaspoon salt
½ teaspoon freshly ground black pepper

1. In a small bowl, combine the beef broth, Worcestershire sauce, soy sauce, brown sugar, onion powder, garlic powder, salt, and pepper until the brown sugar and salt have completely dissolved. Use immediately or make ahead of time and store in an airtight container in the refrigerator for up to 1 week. Bring the mixture to room temperature before using.
2. To use, draw some of the marinade into the injector syringe. Inject small amounts into the roast. Let the meat marinate for at least 30 minutes after injecting and before smoking.

USE WITH: Larger cuts of meat, like beef brisket, chuck roast, prime rib, eye of round, beef plate ribs, and venison roasts.

PORK RIB MARINADE

PREP TIME: 15 minutes

This Spanish-inspired rib marinade is used in *costilla* (rib) recipes. It is best to marinate the ribs for 12 to 24 hours to get the full flavor and tenderizing effect before placing them into the smoker (see SmokeMaster Tip). This recipe makes enough marinade for 3 pounds of pork ribs.

MAKES 1 CUP

½ cup cooking sherry
2 tablespoons tomato paste
Juice of 2 limes
1 tablespoon brown sugar
1 tablespoon soy sauce
¼ cup plus 1 tablespoon olive oil
6 garlic cloves, minced
1 teaspoon salt
½ teaspoon red pepper flakes
½ teaspoon dried oregano
½ teaspoon smoked paprika
½ teaspoon freshly ground black pepper

1. Whisk together the sherry, tomato paste, lime juice, brown sugar, soy sauce, and olive oil in a medium nonreactive bowl (such as glass). Stir in the garlic, salt, red pepper flakes, oregano, paprika, and black pepper until the salt and sugar have dissolved.
2. Use immediately or make ahead of time and store in the fridge for up to 1 week.

SMOKEMASTER TIP: Before marinating the pork ribs, remove the membrane on the back. Place the ribs into a shallow glass baking dish, bone-side down. Pour the marinade over the top, cover the dish with plastic wrap, and refrigerate for 12 to 24 hours. Turn the ribs halfway through the marinating time, cover, and return to the fridge for the remaining time.

QUICK BRINE

PREP TIME: 10 minutes

This is a great all-purpose brine for smaller cuts of meat that require a short brine time. This recipe makes enough brine for 1 pound of meat—double or triple the recipe as needed. To use this Quick Brine, submerge the meat in the brine for 2 hours, lightly rinse under cold water, blot dry with paper towels, then season and cook as directed.

MAKES 1 QUART

4 cups cold water
¼ cup kosher salt
¼ cup white sugar

In a bowl large enough to accommodate both the brine and the meat, combine the water, salt, and sugar and stir until the salt and sugar dissolve.

USE WITH: Small cuts of meat, like chicken breasts, legs, wings, or pork chops and tenderloin. This Quick Brine works great with the Smoky Spatchcock Chicken (page 91), Apricot-Glazed Cornish Game Hens (page 111), and the Steakhouse Pork Chops (page 69).

ALABAMA WHITE SAUCE

PREP TIME: 15 minutes

This slightly sweet, tangy white barbecue sauce is the brainchild of Bob Gibson of Big Bob Gibson's BBQ in Decatur, Alabama. It is not a basting sauce but a finishing sauce served at the table along with smoked chicken pieces. It is excellent in pulled chicken sandwiches.

MAKES 3 CUPS

- 2¼ cups mayonnaise
- 1 teaspoon mustard
- ⅔ cup apple cider vinegar, plus more if desired
- 3 tablespoons freshly squeezed lemon juice
- 2 garlic cloves, minced (or ¼ teaspoon granulated garlic)
- 2 teaspoons prepared horseradish
- 2 teaspoons white sugar
- ½ teaspoon salt
- ½ teaspoon freshly ground black pepper
- ¼ teaspoon cayenne pepper

1. In a medium bowl, combine the mayonnaise, mustard, apple cider vinegar, and lemon juice. Add the garlic, horseradish, sugar, salt, pepper, and cayenne, and stir together until smooth. If you'd like a thinner sauce, add a few tablespoons more apple cider vinegar to the mixture.
2. Serve immediately or store in the refrigerator for up to 10 days.

USE WITH: Smoked whole chicken or chicken pieces, shredded chicken, or smoked, grilled, or pulled turkey.

BLOOD ORANGE BBQ SAUCE

PREP TIME: 10 minutes **/ Cook time:** 10 minutes

The blood orange has a distinctive flavor and yields a bright red juice. The flavor is mellow and sweet and blends well in tomato-based barbecue sauces. If you can't find blood oranges, use four Valencia or Cara Cara oranges.

MAKES 1 TO 1¼ CUPS

- Juice of 2 blood oranges
- Juice of 2 large oranges, such as Valencia or Cara Cara
- ½ cup maple syrup
- 2 teaspoons bourbon
- ⅓ cup ketchup
- 2 tablespoons butter
- 2 teaspoons soy sauce
- ½ teaspoon mild chili powder
- Pinch salt
- Pinch freshly ground black pepper

1. In a medium saucepan over medium heat, combine the blood orange juice, other orange juice, and maple syrup. Simmer for 2 minutes, stirring often.
2. Add the bourbon and let the sauce simmer for an additional minute, then add the ketchup, butter, soy sauce, chili powder, salt, and pepper. Reduce the heat to low and simmer for an additional 5 to 7 minutes. The sauce will start to thicken and take on the consistency of syrup. Remove from heat, cover, and keep warm. If making the sauce for later use, cool completely and store in the refrigerator for up to 1 week.

USE WITH: Pork belly; pork ribs, chops, and tenderloin; chicken and other poultry.

PINEAPPLE SOY GLAZE

PREP TIME: 10 **minutes / Cook time:** 10 minutes

This flavorful pineapple teriyaki-style glaze can be used as a topping sauce or glaze for Double Smoked Ham (page 76) and other meats or seafood items that benefit from a touch of sweetness. The best part about this glaze is that it caramelizes on the surface of the meat as it cooks, giving it a candied flavor.

MAKES 1 CUP

- 1 cup pineapple juice
- ¾ cup light brown sugar
- 2 tablespoons honey
- 1 tablespoon soy sauce
- 1½ teaspoons chili-garlic sauce
- 1 teaspoon grated fresh ginger
- 1 teaspoon rice wine vinegar
- ¼ teaspoon allspice

1. In a medium saucepan over medium-high heat, combine the pineapple juice, brown sugar, honey, soy sauce, chili-garlic sauce, ginger, rice wine vinegar, and allspice and bring it to a simmer, stirring often. Reduce the heat to medium-low and let the sauce continue to simmer for an additional 5 to 7 minutes, or until it starts to thicken and reduce. When it's done, it will have the consistency of syrup.
2. Remove the sauce from heat, cover, and keep warm if using immediately. If making ahead of time, cool the sauce completely and store in an airtight container in the refrigerator for up to 1 week.

USE WITH: Pork roasts, pork belly, ham, poultry, beef, fish, seafood, and vegetables.

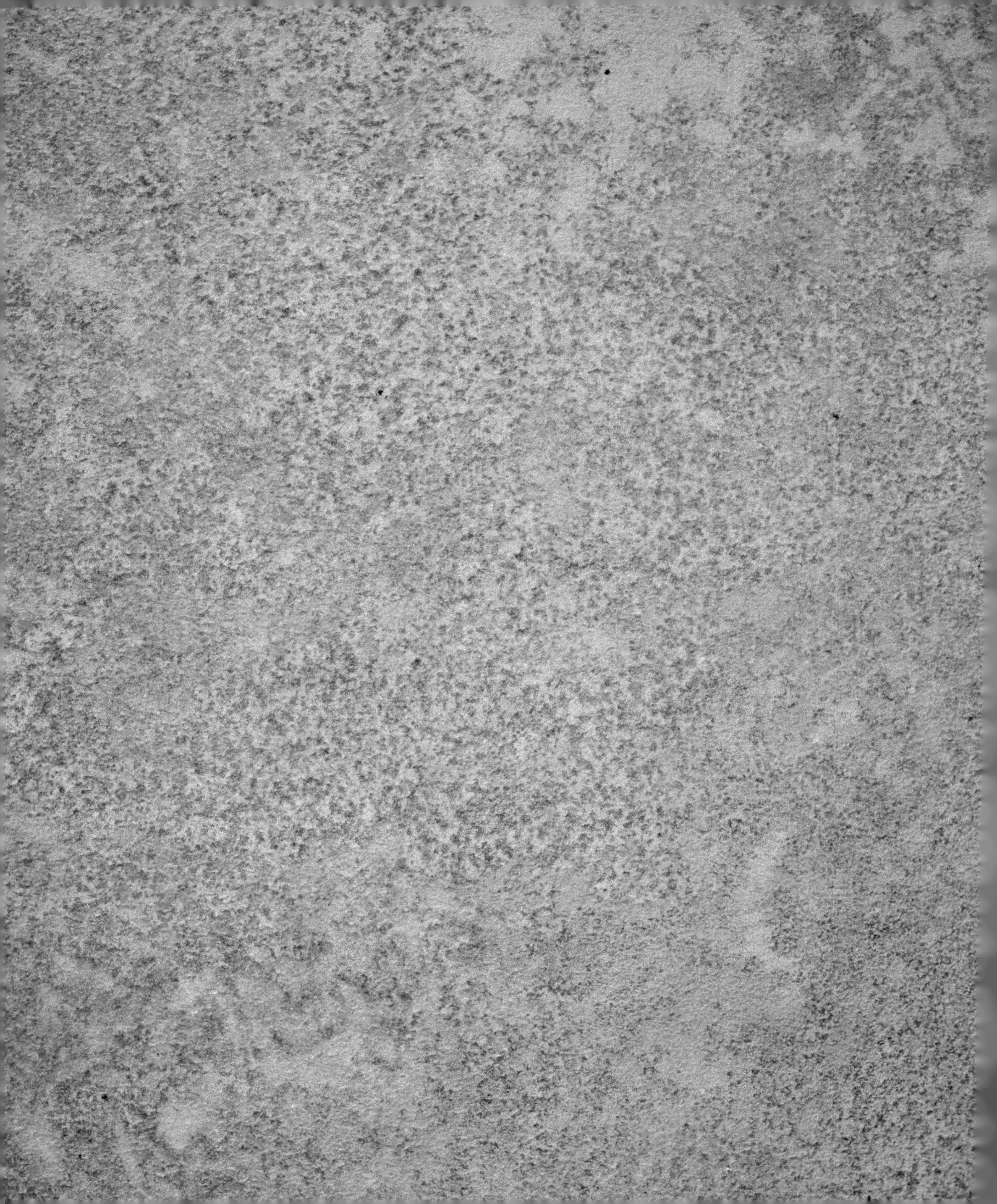

MEASUREMENT CONVERSIONS

VOLUME EQUIVALENTS	U.S. STANDARD	U.S. STANDARD (OUNCES)	METRIC (APPROXIMATE)
LIQUID	2 tablespoons	1 fl. oz.	30 mL
	¼ cup	2 fl. oz.	60 mL
	½ cup	4 fl. oz.	120 mL
	1 cup	8 fl. oz.	240 mL
	1½ cups	12 fl. oz.	355 mL
	2 cups or 1 pint	16 fl. oz.	475 mL
	4 cups or 1 quart	32 fl. oz.	1 L
	1 gallon	128 fl. oz.	4 L
DRY	⅛ teaspoon		0.5 mL
	¼ teaspoon		1 mL
	½ teaspoon		2 mL
	¾ teaspoon		4 mL
	1 teaspoon		5 mL
	1 tablespoon		15 mL
	¼ cup		59 mL
	⅓ cup		79 mL
	½ cup		118 mL
	⅔ cup		156 mL
	¾ cup		177 mL
	1 cup		235 mL
	2 cups or 1 pint		475 mL
	3 cups		700 mL
	4 cups or 1 quart		1 L
	½ gallon		2 L
	1 gallon		4 L

OVEN TEMPERATURES

FAHRENHEIT	CELSIUS (APPROXIMATE)
250°F	120°C
300°F	150°C
325°F	165°C
350°F	180°C
375°F	190°C
400°F	200°C
425°F	220°C
450°F	230°C

WEIGHT EQUIVALENTS

U.S. STANDARD	METRIC (APPROXIMATE)
½ ounce	15 g
1 ounce	30 g
2 ounces	60 g
4 ounces	115 g
8 ounces	225 g
12 ounces	340 g
16 ounces or 1 pound	455 g

INDEX

C

Q

R

S

T

W

ACKNOWLEDGMENTS

We want to thank Rockridge Press and their staff for the opportunity, particularly Anna Pulley, whose editorial guidance helped bring this book to fruition.

ABOUT THE AUTHORS

Sabrina Baksh is a cookbook author, recipe developer, content editor, industry coach, and photographer. Her work has appeared in various online and print venues, including *Esquire* magazine's *The Biggest Black Book Ever,* The Spruce (formerly About.com), and SIDEBARS Australia. She has traveled both nationally and internationally, exploring flavors, cultures, and food history. Sabrina earned a graduate degree in history, which proves indispensable in drawing connections between food traditions. Very passionate about food, flavor, and writing, she takes great joy in the creative process. She recently relocated to Austin, Texas, to explore its rich food culture and experience Texas barbecue to its fullest.

Derrick Riches is a highly respected barbecue and grilling journalist, outdoor cooking expert, and industry consultant. He is best known for his influential site on About.com between 1997 and 2017. He has traveled the world, grilled on almost every conceivable type of cooking equipment, led classes, and judged the best barbecue in the world.

In 2017, he founded a new informational resource at DerrickRiches.com, branded BGDR (Barbecue and Grilling with Derrick Riches). His work remains prominent, particularly in his thought-provoking articles, engaging videos, and notoriously honest product reviews.

Riches has been featured in *The Wall Street Journal,* Huffington Post, the BBC, *The Washington Post,* and numerous books. He has served as a spokesperson for the Hearth, Patio, and Barbecue Association and regularly appears on industry-related podcasts, webcasts, and radio programs. He currently resides in Austin, Texas.

CPSIA information can be obtained
at www.ICGtesting.com
Printed in the USA
LVHW011256271221
706934LV00004B/6